AF266214

In the Garden of Remembrance

IN THE GARDEN OF REMEMBRANCE

A collection of prayers to brighten your heart, ease your burdens, and bathe you in the fragrance of faith

Based on

al-Adhkār al-Murādiyah

li naylin-niʿamil-marḍiyah, wa dafʿil-balāyal-muʿādiyah

By Murād Mujāhid al-Ashʿarī al-ʿAdnānī

Translated and supplemented by
Nishat Aisha Lal

All Rights Reserved © 2026 by Daybreak Press, first published in 2022.

No part of this book may be reproduced or transmitted in any form or by any means, graphic, electronic or mechanical, including photocopying, recording, typing, or by any information storage retrieval system, without the permission of the publisher.

Daybreak Press
3533 Lexington Avenue North, Arden Hills, MN 55126
www.rabata.org/daybreakpress | daybreakpress@rabata.org

ISBN (print): 978-0-9906259-6-4
ISBN (ebook): 978-0-9906259-9-5
LCCN: 2026939894

Cover design: Reyhana Ismail | Reyoflightdesign.com
Design and typesetting: scholarlytype.com

Printed in the United States of America

Contents

Foreword

All praises belong to Allah, the Most Forgiving, the Most Generous. May the peace and blessings of Almighty Allah be upon our noble and beloved Messenger, guide, and teacher, Muḥammad, his family, and his followers.

For centuries, scholars have compiled collections of the supplications of the pious predecessors. In them, they found perfumed breezes carrying the spiritual experiences and emotions of the great men and women of the past. These collections helped connect them to the purity of the earliest generations of Islam and inspired them in their own addresses to God.

Murād al-ʿAdnānī selected some of the most beautiful and moving supplications from these great compilations and elsewhere, making his collection a treasure-trove for the earnest supplicant.

The book in your hands is based on Murād al-ʿAdnānī's collection of beautiful prayers. I have divided the prayers into praises, forgiveness, protection, and personal need, and have added a selection of prayers used at Rabata events as well. I have included Murād al-ʿAdnānī's introduction on the importance of *dhikr* (the remembrance of God) which relies on Quranic verses as well as prophetic traditions and the sayings of pious people, and included his poem speaking about the relationship between God and His servant.

These prayers give the supplicant a voice with which to approach God in a very genuine and touching way. There are those of us who struggle to know with what words we should praise Allah, or how we should go about seeking forgiveness, or indeed what we should ask for of this world and the next. This collection of prayers gifts the supplicant words with which to praise, ways in which to request God's forgiveness, direction in what to seek protection from, and what to ask for. In this way, it prepares the heart of the supplicant for making her own personal prayer, for which there is a space reserved towards the end.

Murād al-'Adnānī completed his collection in 2009. He was born to a Yemeni father and Moroccan mother in Tangiers, Morocco, where he spent most of his life. He studied at the hands of teachers from the famous Qarawiyyīn University and obtained *ijāzas* in Arabic literature, the *aḥādīth* of Imam Mālik, and Islamic law according to the Mālikī school. He is also a linguist, having studied French and Spanish literature.

After leaving Morocco in 1985, he settled in the UK where he is at the heart of and in the hearts of the Cardiff Muslim community. He is a support, a voice of reason and wisdom, and kindness personified. Many a student of Arabic in Cardiff would have crossed paths with Murād al-'Adnānī, just as I at the age of fourteen did. Murād al-'Adnānī built for me the foundations of my Arabic and it brings me great joy to bring these prayers to the English speaker.

I'm grateful and indebted to my mother, Dr. Sufia Lal, for her efforts in taking me to Murād al-'Adnānī's Arabic classes and for paving the way for my Arabic studies at university and beyond. May Allah reward her and forever keep her in His protection.

I thank my husband, Dr. Samer Dajani, for his support always, and for his time and assistance in reviewing this book.

I would also like to commend Daybreak Press for the important work it is doing in promoting female voices in literary and scholarly works. I am so honored that this book has been published through them, and so grateful for their patience and kindness in seeing this work through.

May Allah reward Murād al-'Adnānī for sharing this precious collection with us and write him and his family and all those who recite from this book amongst those who remember Allah abundantly.

Nishat Aisha Lal

A Note on Du‘ā’ (Supplication)

THE ARABIC WORD *du‘ā’* is usually translated as "supplication," meaning to invoke or petition someone—seeking, desiring, or begging in all earnestness for something they are capable of bestowing.

Allah invites each one of us in the Qur’ān to approach Him with our pleas - whatever they may be - for He says that He is ever-near and will respond to the one who calls upon Him.[1]

The Prophet ﷺ likewise instructed us to ask of Allah, for His bounty is great, and He loves to be asked.[2] If God loves to be asked, then it will make Him all the more pleased for us to ask Him over and over again. It is comforting to our hearts that God does not tire of our requests, however great or small they may be.

The Prophet ﷺ called *du‘ā’* the essence of *‘ibāda* (worship)[3] because the one who makes *du‘ā’* cuts off her hopes from anything other than Allah, and that is the reality of *tawḥīd* (belief in the Oneness of Allah) and sincerity. The one who makes *du‘ā’* also shows that she herself has no power or might and that she is in need of Allah, and this is the essence of servanthood.

Allah has counselled us to beseech Him in private so that we may beseech Him with all humility[4] and pour our hearts out to Him without other considerations. The Prophet ﷺ informed us that every night, in the deepest part of the night (that is the last third), Allah descends to the lowest heaven and asks, "Who is supplicating to Me that I may answer their requests? Who is it that is asking of Me that I may give them? Who is it that is seeking My forgiveness that I may forgive them?"[5]

Likewise, we have been informed of other times which are especially suited for beseeching God, times which we should seize for making supplications. We have months such as Ramadan or special days in the year such as the day of 'Arafa, but we also have regularly occurring opportunities such as when it is raining, after the five daily prayers, between the *adhān* (the first call to prayer) and the *iqāma* (the second call to prayer), when we break our fast, during the last hour before sunset every Friday, or when one is in *sajda* (prostration) - for the *du'ā'* made in *sajda*, our Prophet ﷺ informed us, is a *du'ā'* whose acceptance is imminent.[6]

We have also been advised to face the *qibla* (the direction of prayer) when we make *du'ā'*, and to raise our hands with our palms open. God is too generous, our Prophet ﷺ told us, to send back any outstretched palms empty-handed.[7]

Our Prophet ﷺ advised us to begin our supplications with the praises of Allah. Praises remind us of Who it is that we are imploring and His complete capability in granting our each and every request. Hence, prayers in praise of Allah have been placed at the beginning of this collection.

Our Prophet ﷺ then advised us to send *ṣalawāt* (prayers of praise) upon him before coming to our requests[8], therefore *salawāt* upon the Prophet ﷺ are placed immediately after the praises, before the requests begin.

Allah says in the Qur'ān, "*Ask forgiveness from your Lord, then turn to Him repentant; He will cause the sky to rain abundance on you and give you strength upon strength. Do not turn away, guilty.*"[9] The scholars have told us that seeking forgiveness flings open for us the doors of God's giving. Imam al-Nawawī said that repentance to God is the most important of all the etiquettes of supplication and the very foundation upon which God's acceptance of our supplication is built. Therefore, prayers for forgiveness have been placed before any other requests.

After completing our supplications, the scholars have advised us to send *ṣalawāt* upon the Prophet ﷺ again, for Allah will certainly accept the *ṣalawāt* that we send upon the Prophet before and after our requests, and from His generosity we hope that He will not leave out what comes in between. Therefore, *ṣalawāt* have been repeated at the end as well.

This arrangement of prayers allows for the book to flow as one whole supplication, making it ideal for completion in a single sitting if one should wish.

For women who may find themselves unable to pray for a week each month, or indeed for multiple weeks after childbirth, having a book of supplications to turn to, especially during these times, ensures that those days without the prescribed prayers are not days without worship. *Du'ā'* is an important tool in safeguarding those days from passing by in heedlessness, allowing them instead to serve as a beautiful opportunity for us to delve deeply into this other avenue of intimacy with Allah.

The transliteration system used in this book is the ER (Easily Recited) method, which follows the usual academic transliteration system in most ways, but contains a few key differences designed to make it easier for the reader to correctly pronounce what is being recited in Arabic. Those who are used to the academic transliteration system may find it takes them a little time to get used to the method used here. Those who are not familiar with the academic transliteration system will likely find the ER method easier on the tongue.

Names and footnotes have been rendered in standard academic transliteration.

TRANSLITERATION GUIDE

Transliteration symbol	Corresponding Arabic Letter/Vowel
ʾ	ء ئ ؤ أ
b	ب
t	ت
th	ث
j	ج
ḥ	ح
kh	خ
d	د
dh	ذ
r	ر
z	ز

s	س
sh	ش
ṣ	ص
ḍ	ض
ṭ	ط
dh	ظ
ʿ	ع
gh	غ
f	ف
q	ق
k	ك
l	ل
m	م
n	ن
h	ه
w	و
y	ي
a	Short vowel ´
u	Short vowel ʾ
i	Short vowel ˏ
ā	Long vowel ا or ىٰ
ū	Long vowel و
ī	Long vowel ي

In the Garden of Remembrance

INTRODUCTION

In the name of Allah, the Lord of Mercy, the Giver of Mercy.

PRAISE BE TO ALLAH Who does not forget the one who remembers Him: *"So remember Me; I will remember you,"*[10] and Who does not show anger toward the one who persists in calling Him: *"Call on Me, and I will answer you,"*[11] and Who made the obedient as well as the sinner crave His clemency and mercy: *"Say (O Prophet): My servants who have harmed yourselves by your own excess, do not despair of Allah's mercy. Allah forgives all sins, He is truly the Most Forgiving, the Most Merciful."*[12] He is the One Who encourages the believer to keep himself distant from the trait of the hypocrites: *"Little do they hold Allah in remembrance"*[13], *"So woe to those whose hearts are hardened against the remembrance of Allah!"*[14] May the blessings of Allah be upon the master of those who remember Allah and the highest extoller amongst the servants of Allah and the answered of those who supplicate; Sayyidinā Muḥammad, the Messenger of Allah, and upon his family and all of his companions.

How fortunate and intelligent amongst those men and women who remember Allah are those who know how to summon the majesty of Allah in all their affairs, and who know how to be creative in their appeals for Allah's help and their appeals for divine forgiveness! Whenever they expose themselves to the divine breezes, they are able, by the grace of Allah, to vanquish the devils that were swarming between their eyes and which were preventing them from looking to the realms of Allah ﷻ. Through them was fulfilled the saying of Allah's Messenger ﷺ "The *mufarridūn* (forerunners/unique ones) have gone ahead!" The Companions asked, "Who are the *mufarridūn*, O Messenger of Allah?" He replied, "They are those men and women who remember Allah much."[15] We learn from this that Allah ﷻ loves for His servant to praise Him abundantly with exaltation, appreciation, and admiration. Pertaining to this, the Holder of Two Lights, our master ʿUthmān ؓ said, "Even if our hearts were cleansed, we would still not tire from the remembrance of Allah ﷻ."[16]

The Messenger of Allah ﷺ mentioned the description of these people in his saying, "Whenever they are looked upon, Allah is remembered."[17]

How profound and affectionate were our pious predecessors to their kin and brothers and sisters in faith when they clarified the worth of the remembrance of Allah! They said that those whose speech is other than the remembrance of Allah, then they have spoken nonsense, and those whose sight is without profound consideration, then they have been negligent, and those whose silence is without thought, then they have been heedless.

How excellent was Imam 'Alī ﷺ when he said, "Allah, Glorified is He, does not inspire the seeking of forgiveness in a servant of His if He wishes to punish him." That is, the seeking of forgiveness with an aching heart, sincerity of action, and the adherence to the sunnah.

A person has been heedless and negligent who thinks that remembrance is restricted to the tongue alone, for the remembrance of the tongue is exaltation, the remembrance of the eyes is weeping, the remembrance of the ears is attentiveness, the remembrance of the hands is giving, the remembrance of the body is obedience and prophetic emulation, the remembrance of the heart is fearing Allah and placing hopes in Him, and the remembrance of the soul is its submission and contentment. The delight of remembrance is not tasted except by those who take Allah as their companion and leave the people aside.

Mālik ibn Dīnār spoke the truth when he said, "Whoever does not like to take as his companion the speech of Allah ﷻ compared to the speech of His creatures, then he has ruined his deeds, his heart has become blind, and he has squandered his life."

It amazed me that one of the scholars amongst the knowers of Allah deduced that plenty of remembrance was actually a condition for the acceptance of prayer. This is taken from the words of Allah in a hadith *qudsī*, "Indeed, I only accept the prayer of one who... breaks up his day in My remembrance."[18]

As for Allah's saying ﷻ "When you have finished the prayer, then remember Allah standing, sitting, and lying on your sides,"[19] Ibn 'Abbās ﷺ said, "That is in the night and in the day, on land and on the sea, whilst travelling and when settled, in richness and in poverty, in sickness and in health, in secret and in public."

This reminds me of the remark of one of the knowers of Allah when he said, "Indeed on earth there is a paradise, and whoever does not enter it will not enter the paradise of the Hereafter!" He was asked, "And where is it?" He said, "The remembrance of Allah!"

One day, Abū Hurayra ﷺ was passing through the market and he saw people immersed in greed and love of this world, so he said to them, "You are here whilst the inheritance of the Messenger of Allah ﷺ is being distributed in the mosque?!" So they rushed to the mosque but did not find what they desired, so they returned to him and said, "We did not find what you spoke of!" He retorted, "Then what did you find?" They said, "We saw the circles of remembrance." He said to them, "That is the inheritance of the Messenger of Allah ﷺ!"[20]

Imam al-Qurṭubī said, "A gathering of remembrance means a gathering of knowledge and reminding. They are gatherings in which the words of Allah, the sunnah of His Messenger ﷺ and the traditions of the pious predecessors are mentioned."

I add to this that they are those gatherings which nurture the personality of the Muslim - his attitude and his mentality - and make him work to uphold the Law of Allah on earth with conviction, proof, gentleness, and with the aid of the intelligent amongst the influential people of this ummah.

Abū al-Dardā' ﷺ said, "Those whose tongues are constantly moist with the remembrance of Allah will enter

Paradise laughing."[21] Glad tidings to these men and women who remember Allah, for their hearts are not malevolent, their chests are not full of hatred, and their souls are not distant from one another. Their Lord has cascaded them with overflowing goodness and poured forth upon them showers of blessings. They revel in the garden of remembrance and they climb the ascents of divine honor. He ﷺ said, "Whoever wishes to revel in the Garden of Paradise should increase in the remembrance of Allah ﷻ."[22]

These men and women who remember Allah are provided with divine care and surrounded with God's grace. Their Lord protects them from the misguided people who work on suspicions and follow the course of their desires, just as He ﷻ protects them from the evil of false gods who prepare falsehood for every truth and death for every life!

Al-Fuḍayl ؓ used to say about the statement of Allah ﷻ *"And do not kill yourselves,"*[23] that it means do not neglect yourselves and do not forget the remembrance of Allah in all your states, for whoever neglects His remembrance has killed himself! This is what the tradition of the Messenger of Allah ﷺ alludes to when he said, "The likeness of the one who remembers Allah and the one who does not remember Allah is like the living and the dead."[24] He ﷺ also said, "The one who remembers Allah amongst those who are heedless is like the warrior amongst those who are fleeing."[25]

Mu'ādh ibn Jabal ؓ said, "There is no deed which will save one from the punishment of Allah more than the remembrance of Allah." The Messenger of Allah ﷺ said, "Shall I not tell you what is the best of all your deeds, which will raise you the highest in rank, is the purest in the sight of your King, is better for you than giving gold and silver in charity, and better for you than meeting your enemies in battle and striking them and being struck by them?" They said, "Yes." He said, "The remembrance of Allah."[26]

It was narrated of the pious predecessors that they said every soul leaves this world thirsty except for the one who remembers Allah ﷻ. It is mentioned from them ﷺ that they said that two grants of security were given on earth from the punishment of Allah, and that one of them has been lifted whilst the other remains. The first was Sayyidinā Muḥammad ﷺ and the second is the seeking of forgiveness.

This is how the pious predecessors were; it hurt them that a moment from their life should be lost or that a breath of theirs should escape from them in heedlessness or frivolity or indeed anything in which lies no benefit.

So contemplate what I have found in terms of advice from the pious predecessors to those who come after them; it is that the true Muslim is the one who holds his tongue back except from the remembrance of Allah ﷻ or from a good thing which he is clarifying, or a falsehood which he is refuting, or knowledge which he is spreading, or a blessing which he is mentioning.

It is mentioned in the *Muwaṭṭa'* of Imam Mālik (the earliest written collection of *aḥādīth*) that Jesus ﷺ used to say, "Do not be abundant in speech devoid of the remembrance of Allah, for your hearts will become hardened, and indeed the hard heart is distant from Allah, but you do not know." This is a warning to those preachers who spread knowledge amongst the people but when in solitude they seldom remember Allah. The *umma* will not benefit from their knowledge and they will have no positive effect on society!

A poet said:

> When the hidden and the open are equivalent to a believer
> Then he has achieved victory in both worlds and is worthy of both
> And if his hidden deeds are contrary to his open deeds
> Then there is nothing for him in either world except trouble and distress.

Some of the knowers of Allah have said, "When you speak, know that Allah hears you, and when you are silent, know that He sees you!"

As for supplication, which is the essence of worship, the core of remembrance, and the fortress of a believer, it is considered a reason for the attainment of mercy and the dispelling of afflictions, just as a shield is the reason behind warding off an arrow and water is the reason for the growth of plants, as al-Ghazālī ﷺ said. There is nothing nobler in the sight of Allah than supplication, and the Messenger of Allah ﷺ was one who supplicated a lot, and he guided his companions and the *umma* to seek help for all their needs through remembrance and supplication in ease and in difficulty. This is what he himself ﷺ did in the most difficult and severe situations. At Uḥud, after his army was defeated, his companions were slaughtered, his uncle was maimed, and his canine tooth was broken, he said to his companions, "Form rows behind me that I may praise my Lord."[27] O Messenger of Allah, my eyes have never seen the likes of You, and indeed women have not given birth to the likes of You!

Before battle, it was his habit ﷺ to gather the poor, the orphans, and the widows, and say to them, "We are going towards that which you can see, so invoke Allah for us that He may grant us victory," whilst he himself was the infallible one whose supplication was always answered! He said, "Indeed, you are granted victory and provided for due to the weak amongst you."[28]

When the Prophet of Allah Sulaymān ﷺ prayed for rain with his people, he passed an ant on its back with its legs raised to the sky, and it was saying, "O Allah, indeed we are one of Your creatures, and we cannot do without Your sustenance, so do not cause us to perish due to the sins of others!" So Sulaymān ﷺ said to his people, "Go back, for you have been granted rain by the supplication of others!"

How astonishing are the ones who sustain themselves with that which is unlawful - with money from interest, illegal possessions, and the property of others. How many they are today! They wait impatiently for rain as if it is long overdue but, in reality, it is *stones* falling down from the sky that are long overdue!

O Allah, assist the one who does not own anything but supplication, and whose only weapon is his tears, and whose capital is his hope! O Allah, You have shown us Your might on many occasions, so show us Your mercy, O Most Merciful of those who show mercy!

Supplication produces blessed fruits in the future as well as in the present. It has been narrated in a report that one of three things must happen to a servant based on his supplication: a sin is forgiven for him, some good is hastened to him, or some good is stored for him.

These supplications and formulas of remembrance are more beneficial than desperately awaited rain! They were mentioned by people who did not allow their eyes the luxury of slumber and whose supplications and formulas of remembrance of God would not only cause the heavens to burst forth with their waters and the valleys to be abundant with their copiously flowing streams, but were also characterized by the beauty of brocade and would directly touch the soul.

These people were truly lighthouses on the horizons. They are the pride of all time! I swear they deserve to be called lanterns for the believers in these miserable and heavy days. May God have mercy on those whose hearts gained gnosis and so their eyes flowed forth with tears!

I have extracted this selection of formulas of remembrance and supplications from the depths of some of the most important books and have adopted them as a way of life as much as I can. I have made them a compulsory litany for my every day. In them is cure for one exhausted by (spiritual, mental, and physical) illness. I ask Allah, the Forbearing, to benefit my family and all of the Muslims by them. Indeed, remembrance of Allah and supplication are two lifelines toward salvation.

May the blessings of Allah be upon the leader of all those who remember Allah and supplicate to Him: Muḥammad, the messenger of Allah, and his pure family and his choicest companions.

Murād al-ʿAdnānī

PRAISES

• 1 •

سُبْحَانَ اللهِ وَبِحَمْدِهِ سُبْحَانَ اللهِ الْعَظِيم

Subḥānal-lāhi wa bi ḥamdihi subḥānal-lāhil-'a<u>dh</u>īm.

Glory and praise be to Allah, Glory be to Allah the
Magnificent.[29]

• 2 •

سُبْحَانَ اللهِ وَالْحَمْدُ لِلهِ وَلَا إِلٰهَ إِلَّا اللهُ وَاللهُ أَكْبَرُ

*Subḥānal-lāhi wal-ḥamdu lil-lāhi wa lā ilāha illal-lāhu
wal-lāhu akbar.*

Glory be to Allah, praise be to Allah, there is no God but
Allah, and Allah is the Greatest.[30]

• 3 •

سُبْحَانَ اللهِ وَبِحَمْدِهِ عَدَدَ خَلْقِهِ وَرِضَا نَفْسِهِ وَزِنَةَ عَرْشِهِ وَمِدَادَ كَلِمَاتِهِ

*Subḥānal-lāhi wa biḥamdihi ʿadada khalqihi wa riḍā nafsihi
wa zinata ʿarshihi wa midāda kalimātih.*

Glory and praise be to Allah as many times as the number
of His creatures, to the extent of His pleasure, equal to the
weight of His Throne, and to the amount of ink required
for His words.[31]

• 4 •

*سُبْحَانَكَ مَا أَعْظَمَ شَأْنَكَ سُبْحَانَكَ مَا أَعْظَمَ مَا نَرَىٰ مِنْ خَلْقِكَ، مَا أَسْبَغَ
نِعَمِكَ فِي الدُّنْيَا، وَمَا أَصْغَرَهَا فِي نِعَمِ الْآخِرَةِ*

*Subḥānaka mā a<u>dh</u>ama shaʾnaka subḥānaka mā a<u>dh</u>ama
mā narā min khalqik, mā asbagha niʿamika fid-dunyā, wa
mā aṣgharahā fī niʿamil-ākhirah.*

Glory be to You, how Magnificent are You! Glory be to You,
how magnificent is what we see of Your creation! How abundant are Your blessings in this world and how small are they
in comparison to the blessings of the next world![32]

• 5 •

* يَا رَبِّ لَكَ الْحَمْدُ كَمَا يَنْبَغِي لِجَلَالِ وَجْهِكَ وَعَظِيمِ سُلْطَانِكَ *

*Yā rabbi lakal-ḥamdu kamā yambaghī lijalāli wajhika wa
'a<u>dh</u>īmi sulṭānik.*

Praise be to You, my Lord, as is befitting the majesty of Your
countenance and the might of Your sovereignty. [33]

• 6 •

*لَا إِلٰهَ إِلَّا اللهُ وَحْدَهُ لَا شَرِيكَ لَهُ، لَهُ الْمُلْكُ وَلَهُ الْحَمْدُ يُحْيِي وَيُمِيتُ بِيَدِهِ الْخَيْرُ وَهُوَ عَلَىٰ كُلِّ شَيْءٍ قَدِيرٌ *

*Lā ilāha illal-lāhu waḥdahu lā sharīka lah, lahul-mulku wa
lahul-ḥamd, yuḥyī wa yumīt, bi yadihil-khayr, wa huwa 'alā
kulli shay'in qadīr.*

There is no God except Allah alone; He has no partner. To
Him belongs the dominion and to Him belongs all praise. All
goodness lies in His hands—He grants life, He causes death,
and He possesses mastery over everything. [34]

• 7 •

اَللّٰهُمَّ أَنْتَ أَحَقُّ مَنْ ذُكِرَ وَأَحَقُّ مَنْ عُبِدَ، الْحَلَالُ مَا أَحْلَلْتَ وَالْحَرَامُ مَا حَرَّمْتَ، وَالدِّينُ مَا شَرَعْتَ، وَالْأَمْرُ مَا قَضَيْتَ*

*Allāhumma anta aḥaqqu man dhukira wa aḥaqqu man ʿubid,
al-ḥalālu mā aḥlalta wal-ḥarāmu mā ḥarramta wad-dīnu
mā sharaʿta wal-amru mā qaḍayt.*

O Allah, You are the most worthy of being remembered and
the most deserving of being worshipped. The lawful is that
which You have made lawful and the unlawful is that which
You have made unlawful. The religion is that which You have
prescribed, and the command is as You have decreed.[35]

• 8 •

آمَنْتُ بِاللهِ الْوَاحِدِ الْأَحَدِ، وَكَفَرْتُ بِالْجِبْتِ وَالطَّاغُوتِ، وَاسْتَمْسَكْتُ بِالْعُرْوَةِ الْوُثْقَىٰ لَا انْفِصَامَ لَهَا، وَاللهُ سَمِيعٌ عَلِيمٌ

*Āmantu bil-lāhil-wāḥidil-aḥad, wa kafartu bil-jibti
waṭ-ṭāghūt, was-tamsaktu bil-ʿurwatil-wuthqā lan-fiṣāma
lahā, wal-lāhu samīʿun ʿalīm.*

I believe in Allah the One and Only. I reject idols and false gods, and I have seized the firm tie which will never be broken. Allah is All-Hearing, All-Knowing.[36]

• 9 •

رَضِيتُ بِاللهِ رَبًّا، وَبِالْإِسْلَامِ دِينًا، وَبِمُحَمَّدٍ صَلَّى اللهُ عَلَيْهِ وَسَلَّمَ نَبِيًّا وَرَسُولًا*

Raḍītu bil-lāhi rabbā, wa bil-islāmi dīnā, wa bi Muḥammadin ṣallal-lāhu ʿalayhi wa sallama nabiyyan wa rasūlā.

I am pleased with Allah as my Lord, with Islam as my way of life, and with Muhammad ﷺ as my prophet and messenger.[37]

• 10 •

اَللّٰهُمَّ مَنْ عَرَفَكَ ذَهَلَ فُؤَادُهُ فِي مَلَكُوتِكَ يَا أَعَزَّ مَنْ دُعِيَ وَأَكْرَمَ مَنْ أَجَابَ*

Allāhumma man ʿarafaka dhahala fuʾāduhu fī malakūtika yā aʿazza man duʿiya wa akrama man ajāb.

O Allah, whoever comes to know You, his heart is enchanted by Your kingdom! O Most Powerful of those who are called upon and Most Generous of those who oblige.

• 11 •

يَا اللهُ سُبْحَانَكَ، مَنِ الَّذِي عَامَلَكَ فَلَمْ يَرْبَحْ، مَنِ الَّذِي الْتَجَأَ إِلَيْكَ فَلَمْ يَفْرَحْ، لَا خَيْرَ يُرْجَىٰ إِلَّا فِي يَدَيْكَ

Yā Allāhu subḥānak, manil-ladhī ʿāmalaka fa lam yarbaḥ, manil-ladhil-tajaʾa ilayka fa lam yafraḥ, lā khayra yurjā illā fī yadayk.

O Allah, glory be to You, who is it that trades with You and does not profit? Who is it that takes refuge in You and does not rejoice? No good is sought except from Your hands.[38]

• 12 •

يَا كَثِيرَ الْخَيْرِ يَا دَائِمَ الْمَعْرُوف

Yā kathīral-khayri yā dāʾimal-maʿrūf!

O One of much goodness, O One of infinite kindness![39]

ṢALAWĀT

(Lauding the Prophet ﷺ)

• 13 •

ٱللّٰهُمَّ صَلِّ عَلَىٰ سَيِّدِنَا مُحَمَّدٍ، صَلَاةً تُخْرِجُنَا بِهَا يَا اللهُ مِنْ ظُلُمَاتِ الْوَهْمِ وَتُكْرِمُنَا بِهَا بِنُورِ الْفَهْمِ، وَتَهَبُ لَنَا بِهَا أَكْمَلَ الْمُرَادِ فِي دَارِ الدُّنْيَا وَالْمَعَادِ

Allāhumma ṣalli ʿalā sayyidinā Muḥammad, ṣalātan tukhrijunā bihā yā Allāhu min dhulumātil-wahmi wa tukrimunā bihā binūril-fahmi wa tahabu lanā bihā akmalal-murādi fī dārid-dunyā wal-maʿād.

O Allah, bless Sayyidinā Muhammad a blessing through which You remove us from the darkness of delusion, and through which You honor us with the light of understanding, and through which You grant us everything we wish for in this life and the next.

• 14 •

اَللّٰهُمَّ صَلِّ عَلَىٰ سَيِّدِنَا مُحَمَّدٍ، طِبِّ الْقُلُوبِ وَدَوَائِهَا، وَعَافِيَةِ الْأَبْدَانِ وَشِفَائِهَا، وَنُورِ الْأَبْصَارِ وَضِيَائِهَا، وَعَلَىٰ آلِهِ وَصَحْبِهِ وَسَلِّمْ

Allāhumma ṣalli ʿalā sayyidinā Muḥammad, ṭibbil-qulūbi wa dawāʾihā, wa ʿāfiyatil-abdāni wa shifāʾihā, wa nūril-abṣāri wa ḍiyāʾihā, wa ʿalā ālihi wa ṣaḥbihi wa sallim.

O Allah, bless Sayyidinā Muhammad, the medicine of our hearts and their cure, the health of our bodies and their healing, and the light of our eyes and their illumination.[40]

Forgiveness

• 15 •

أَسْتَغْفِرُ اللهَ الْعَظِيمَ وَأَتُوبُ إِلَيْهِ

Astaghfirul-lāhal-ʿadhīm wa atūbu ilayh.

I seek forgiveness from Allah the Magnificent and I repent to Him.[41]

• 16 •

لَا إِلَهَ إِلَّا أَنْتَ سُبْحَانَكَ إِنِّي كُنْتُ مِنَ الظَّالِمِينَ

Lā ilāha illā anta subḥānaka innī kuntu minadh-dhālimīn.

There is no God but You, glory be to You, truly I have been of those who do wrong. [42]

• 17 •

اَللّٰهُمَّ أَنْتَ رَبِّی لَا إِلٰهَ إِلَّا أَنْتَ خَلَقْتَنِي وَأَنَا عَبْدُكَ وَأَنَا عَلَىٰ عَهْدِكَ وَوَعْدِكَ مَا اسْتَطَعْتُ أَعُوذُ بِكَ مِنْ شَرِّ مَا صَنَعْتُ أَبُوءُ لَكَ بِنِعْمَتِكَ عَلَيَّ وَأَبُوءُ بِذَنْبِي فَاغْفِرْلِی فَإِنَّهُ لَا يَغْفِرُ الذُّنُوبَ إِلَّا أَنْتَ

Allāhumma anta rabbī lā ilāha illā anta khalaqtanī wa ana 'abduka wa ana 'alā 'ahdika wa wa'dika mas-taṭa'tu a'ūdhu bika min sharri mā ṣana'tu abū'u laka bi ni'matika 'alayya wa abū'u bi dhambī fagh-firlī fa innahu lā yaghfirudh-dhunūba illā ant.

O Allah, You are my Lord, there is no God but You. You created me, I am Your servant, and I remain faithful to my covenant with You and my promise to You as much as I can. I seek refuge in You from the evil that I have committed. I acknowledge before You the blessings You have bestowed upon me and I acknowledge my sins, so forgive me, for truly no one forgives sins except You.[43]

• 18 •

اَللّٰهُمَّ اغْفِرْ لِي خَطِيئَتِي وَجَهْلِي وَإِسْرَافِي فِي أَمْرِي، وَمَا أَنْتَ أَعْلَمُ بِهِ مِنِّي

Allāhummagh-fir lī khaṭī'atī wa jahlī wa isrāfī fī amrī, wa mā anta a'lamu bihi minnī.

O Allah, forgive me for my mistakes, my ignorance, my
wastefulness in my affairs, and for those things in me which
You are more knowledgeable about than I.[44]

• 19 •

اَللّٰهُمَّ إِنَّ ذُنُوْئِ وَإِنْ كَثُرَتْ وَجَلَّتْ عَنِ الصِّفَة، فَإِنَّهَا صَغِيرَةٌ فِي جَنْبِ عَفْوِكَ فَاعْفُ عَنِّي

*Allāhumma inna dhunūbī wa in kathurat wa jallat ‘aniṣ-ṣifah,
fa’innahā ṣaghīratun fī janbi ‘afwika fa‘-fu ‘annī.*

O Allah, even if my sins are too many and too great to describe,
they are small when placed beside Your pardon, so pardon
me.[45]

• 20 •

اَللّٰهُمَّ أَدْخِلْ عَظِيمَ جُرْمِي فِي عَظِيمِ عَفْوِكَ يَا أَرْحَمَ الرَّاحِمِينَ

*Allāhumma adkhil ‘aḏhīma jurmī fī ‘aḏhīmi ‘afwika yā
arḥamar-rāḥimīn.*

O Allah, engulf my vast crimes with Your vast pardon, O
Most Merciful of those who show mercy.

• 21 •

اَللّٰهُمَّ اجْعَلْنِي مِنْ أَحْبَابِكَ، فَإِنَّكَ إِذَا أَحْبَبْتَ عَبْدًا غَفَرْتَ ذَنْبَهُ وَإِنْ كَانَ عَظِيمًا، وَقَبِلْتَ عَمَلَهُ وَإِنْ كَانَ يَسِيرًا

Allāhummaj-ʿalnī min aḥbābik, faʾinnaka idhā aḥbabta ʿabdan ghafarta dhambahu wa in kāna ʿadhīmā, wa qabilta ʿamalahu wa in kāna yasīrā.

O Allah, make me amongst those who are dear to You, for truly if You love Your servant, You forgive his sins even if they are great, and You accept his good works even if they are few.[46]

• 22 •

اَللّٰهُمَّ إِنَّا لَمْ نَأْتِ الذُّنُوبَ جُرْأَةً مِنَّا عَلَيْكَ وَلَا اسْتِخْفَافًا بِحَقِّكَ، فَالْمَعْذِرَةُ إِلَيْكَ، وَلٰكِنْ سَوَّلَتْ لَنَا أَنْفُسَنَا بِذٰلِكَ، فَارْحَمْنَا وَاغْفِرْ لَنَا يَا أَرْحَمَ الرَّاحِمِينَ

Allāhumma innā lam naʾtidh-dhunūba jurʾatan minnā ʿalayka wa las-tikhfāfan biḥaqqik, fal-maʿdhiratu ilayk, wa lākin sawwalat lanā anfusanā bidhālik, far-ḥamnā wagh-fir lanā yā arḥamar-rāhimīn.

O Allah, truly we do not commit our sins out of insolence towards You nor belittling Your rights upon us, but our lower selves entice us to commit them, so have mercy on us and forgive us, O Most Merciful of those who show mercy.

• 23 •

* يَا مَنْ إِذَا وَعَدَ أَوْفَىٰ وَإِذَا أَوْعَدَ عَفَا، أَسْتَغْفِرُكَ مِنْ كُلِّ ذَنْبٍ تُبْتُ إِلَيْكَ مِنْهُ ثُمَّ عُدْتُ فِيهِ، وَمِنْ كُلِّ عَمَلٍ أَرَدْتُ بِهِ وَجْهَكَ فَخَالَطَهُ غَيْرُكَ، وَأَسْتَغْفِرُكَ مِنْ كُلِّ نِعْمَةٍ أَنْعَمْتَ بِهَا عَلَيَّ فَاسْتَعَنْتُ بِهَا عَلَى مَعْصِيَتِكَ *

Yā man idhā waʿada awfā wa idhā awʿada ʿafā, astaghfiruka min kulli dhanbin tubtu ilayka minhu thumma ʿudtu fīh, wa min kulli ʿamalin aradtu bihi wajhaka fakhālaṭahu ghayruk, wa astaghfiruka min kulli niʿmatin anʿamta bihā ʿalayya fas-taʿantu bihā ʿalā maʿṣiyatik.

O One Who if He promises goodness He fulfills it and if He threatens punishment He waives it, I seek Your forgiveness for every sin for which I repented to You but then reverted to, and for every deed which I intended for Your sake but then mingled other than You in my intention. I seek Your forgiveness for every blessing which You bestowed upon me that I made use of to disobey You.[47]

• 24 •

اَللّٰهُمَّ إِنْ كُنَّا عَصَيْنَاكَ فَقَدْ تَرَكْنَا مِنْ مَعَاصِيكَ أَبْغَضَهَا إِلَيْكَ وَهُوَ الْإِشْرَاكُ، وَإِنْ كُنَّا قَصَّرْنَا عَنْ بَعْضِ طَاعَتِكَ فَقَدْ تَمَسَّكْنَا بِأَحَبِّهَا إِلَيْكَ وَهُوَ التَّوْحِيد

Allāhumma in kunnā ‘aṣaynāka faqad taraknā min ma‘āṣīka abghaḍahā ilayka wa huwal-ishrāk, wa in kunnā qaṣṣarnā ‘an ba‘ḍi ṭā‘atika faqad tamassaknā bi’aḥabbihā ilayka wa huwat-tawḥīd.

O Allah, even though we have disobeyed You, we have left what is most hateful to You of disobedience, which is associating others with You. And even though we have fallen short in some of our obedience to You, we have clung to the most beloved of it to You, which is belief in Your Oneness.[48]

• 25 •

اَللّٰهُمَّ إِنِّي أَذْنَبْتُ فِي بَعْضِ الْأَوْقَاتِ وَآمَنْتُ بِكَ فِي كُلِّ الْأَوْقَاتِ، فَكَيْفَ يَغْلِبُ بَعْضُ عُمْرِي مُذْنِبًا جَمِيعَ عُمْرِي مُؤْمِنًا! فَإِنْ غَفَرْتَ فَخَيْرُ رَاحِمٍ كُنْتَ، وَإِنْ عَذَّبْتَ فَغَيْرُ ظَالِمٍ أَنْتَ

Allāhumma innī adhnabtu fī baʻḍil-awqāti wa āmantu bika fī kullil-awqāti, fa kayfa yaghlibu baʻḍu ʻumrī mudhniban jamīʻa ʻumrī muʼminā! Faʼin ghafarta fa khayru rāḥimin kunt, wa in ʻadhdhabta fa ghayru ḏhālimin ant.

O Allah, truly I have sinned sometimes, but I have believed in You at all times, so how can a fraction of my life as a sinner prevail over my entire life as a believer? If You forgive me, then You are the best of those who show mercy, and if You punish me, then You are not unjust.[49]

• **26** •

اَللّٰهُمَّ لَا تُعْرِضْ عَنِّي يَوْمَ الْعَرْضِ، وَلَا تَخْذِلْنِي بِكَثْرَةِ فَضَائِحِي، أَنَا تَائِبٌ إِلَيْكَ فَاقْبَلْ ذٰلِكَ مِنِّي، وَلَا تَجْعَلْنِي لِنَارِ جَهَنَّمَ وَقُودًا بَعْدَ تَوْحِيدِكَ وَإِيمَانِي بِرَحْمَتِكَ يَا أَرْحَمَ الرَّاحِمِينَ

Allāhumma lā tuʻriḍ ʻannī yawmal-ʻarḍ, wa lā takhdhilnī bikathrati faḍāʼiḥī, ana tāʼibun ilayka faq-bal dhālika minnī, wa lā tajʻalnī lināri jahannama waqūdan baʻda tawḥīdika wa īmānī biraḥmatika yā arḥamar-rāḥimīn.

O Allah, do not turn away from me on the Day of Exposition, and do not abandon me due to the multitude of my shameful acts. I repent to You, so accept my repentance and do not make me fuel for the fire of Hell after I testified to Your Oneness and believed in Your mercy, O Most Merciful of those who show mercy.[50]

• 27 •

اَللّٰهُمَّ اغْفِرْ مَا عَلِمْتَ، وَلَا تَهْتِكْ مَا سَتَرْتَ، إِلٰهَنَا وَرَبَّنَا إِنْ كُنَّا عَصَيْنَاكَ بِجَهْلٍ فَقَدْ دَعَوْنَاكَ بِعَقْلٍ حَيْثُ عَلِمْنَا أَنَّ لَنَا رَبًّا يَغْفِرُ لَنَا وَلَا يُبَالِي. أَتَحْرِقُ بِالنَّارِ وَجْهًا كَانَ لَكَ مُصَلِّيًا، وَلِسَانًا كَانَ لَكَ ذَاكِرًا وَدَاعِيًا، لَا بِالَّذِي دَلَّنَا عَلَيْكَ وَأَمَرَنَا بِالْخُشُوعِ بَيْنَ يَدَيْكَ مُحَمَّدٌ صَلَّى اللهُ عَلَيْهِ وَسَلَّمَ خَاتَمُ أَنْبِيَائِكَ، وَسَيِّدُ أَصْفِيَائِكَ، وَمَعْدِنُ أَسْرَارِكَ، وَعَلَى آلِهِ الْأَطْهَارِ وَأَصْحَابِهِ الْأَخْيَارِ*

Allāhummagh-fir mā ʿalimt, wa lā tahtik mā satart, ilāhanā wa rabbanā in kunnā ʿaṣaynāka bijahlin faqad daʿawnāka biʿaqlin ḥaythu ʿalimnā anna lanā rabban yaghfiru lanā wa lā yubālī. Ataḥriqu bin-nāri wajhan kāna laka muṣalliyā, wa lisānan kāna laka dhākiran wa daʿiyā? Lā bil-ladhī dallanā ʿalayka wa amaranā bil-kushūʿi bayna yadayka Muḥammadin ṣallal-lāhu ʿalayhi wa sallama khātami ambiyāʾik, wa sayyidi aṣfiyāʾik, wa maʿdini asrārik, wa ʿalā ālihil-aṭhāri wa aṣḥābihil-akhyār.

O Allah, forgive what You know and do not reveal what You have concealed. Our Lord, if we disobeyed You out of ignorance, then we are now supplicating to You out of knowledge, for we know that we have a Lord Who will forgive and Who will not mind. Would You burn a face with the Fire which used to prostrate to You? A tongue which used to remember You and supplicate to You? By the one who guided us to You and commanded us to stand humbly before You, Muḥammad, the final seal of Your prophets, the leader of Your chosen ones, the mine of Your secrets, may peace and blessings be upon him, his pure family, and his choicest companions, of course You would not![51]

• 28 •

اَللّٰهُمَّ إِنَّكَ تَسْمَعُ كَلَامِي وَتَرَىٰ مَكَانِي وَتَعْلَمُ سِرِّي وَعَلَانِيَتِي، وَأَنَا الْبَائِسُ الْفَقِيرُ الْمُسْتَغِيثُ الْمُقِرُّ الْمُعْتَرِفُ بِذَنْبِهِ، أَدْعُوكَ دُعَاءَ الْخَائِفِ الضَّرِيرِ مَنْ خَضَعَتْ لَكَ رَقَبَتُهُ وَفَاضَتْ لَكَ عَيْنَاهُ وَرَغَمَ لَكَ أَنْفُهُ. عُبَيْدُكَ فِي فِنَائِكَ، اُنْظُرْ إِلَيَّ وَأَشْفِقْ عَلَيَّ يَا حَلِيمُ يَا وَدُودُ

Allāhumma innaka tasma'u kalāmī wa tarā makānī wa ta'lamu sirrī wa 'alāniyatī, wa anal-bā'is ul-faqīr ul-mustaghīth ul-muqirr ul-mu'tarifu bi dhanbih, ad'ūka du'ā'al-khā'ifiḍ-ḍarīri man khaḍa'at laka raqabatuhu wa fāḍat laka 'aynāhu wa raghama laka anfuh. 'Ubayduka fī finā'ik, undhur ilayya wa ashfiq 'alayya yā ḥalīmu yā wadūd.

O Allah, truly You hear my speech and You see my situation. You know what I hide and what I display. I am a poor, wretched person seeking Your help, acknowledging and admitting my sins. I call out to You with the supplication of a fearful person wandering in darkness, whose neck has humbled itself before You, whose eyes have poured forth before You, and whose nose has humbled itself before You.[52] Your small servant is at Your doorstep; look towards me, have pity on me, O Forbearing One, O Loving One.

• 29 •

رَبَّنَا وَإِلٰهَنَا مَا عَصَيْنَاكَ جَهْلًا بِعِقَابِكَ وَلَا تَعَرُّضًا لِعَذَابِك، لٰكِنْ سَوَّلَتْهَا نُفُوسُنَا، وَأَعَانَتْنَا شَقْوَتُنَا، وَغَرَّنَا سِتْرُكَ عَلَيْنَا، وَأَطْمَعْنَا فِي عَفْوِكَ بِرُّكَ بِنَا، فَبِحَبْلِ مَنْ نَعْتَصِمُ إِنْ قَطَعْتَ حَبْلَكَ عَنَّا. وَاخَجْلَتَاه غَداً مِنَ الْوُقُوفِ بَيْنَ يَدَيْك، وَافَضِيحَتَاه إِنْ عُرِضَتْ أَفْعَالُنَا الْقَبِيحَةَ عَلَيْك.

Rabbanā wa ilāhanā mā ‘aṣaynāka jahlan bi‘iqābika wa lā ta‘arruḍan li ‘adhābik, lākin sawwalat-hā nufūsunā, wa a‘ānatnā shaqwatunā, wa gharranā sitruka ‘alaynā, wa aṭma‘nā fī ‘afwika birruka binā, fabiḥabli man na‘taṣimu in qaṭa‘ta ḥablaka ‘annā. Wā khajlatāh ghadan minal-wuqūfi bayna yadayk, wā faḍīḥatāh in ‘araḍat af‘ālanal-qabīḥata ‘alayk.

Our Lord, we have not disobeyed You out of ignorance of Your punishment, nor seeking to expose ourselves to Your torment, but our lower selves enticed us to it, our misfortune aided us, we allowed Your covering of our faults to make us complacent, and Your goodness toward us made us hold out hopes for Your pardon. So to whose rope do we cling if You cut off Your rope from us? Oh my shame tomorrow from standing in front of You! Oh my humiliation that my ugly deeds will be presented before You!

• 30 •

يَا حَنَّانُ يَا مَنَّانُ إِذَا كَانَتْ رَحْمَتُكَ لِلْمُحْسِنِينَ فَإِلَى أَيْنَ تَذْهَبُ آمَالُ الْمُذْنِبِينَ، أُشْهِدُكَ أَنَّ كُلَّ فَرَحٍ بِغَيْرِكَ زَائِلٌ، وَكُلَّ شُغْلٍ بِسِوَاكَ بَاطِلٌ

Yā ḥannānu yā mannānu idhā kānat raḥmatuka lil-muḥsinīna fa ilā ayna tadhhabu āmālul-mudhnibīn, ushhiduka anna kulla faraḥin bi ghayrika zā'il, wa kulla shughlin bi siwāka bāṭil.

O Affectionate, O Benefactor, if Your mercy is only for those who do good, then where should the hopes of the sinners go? I call upon You to witness my testimony that every joy without You is fleeting and every preoccupation with other than You is in vain.[53]

• 31 •

يَا اللهُ بِأَيِّ رِجْلٍ أَمْشِي إِلَيْكَ، أَمْ بِأَيِّ عَيْنٍ أَنْظُرُ إِلَيْكَ، أَمْ بِأَيِّ لِسَانٍ أُنَاجِيكَ، أَمْ بِأَيِّ يَدٍ أَدْعُوكَ، لَكِنِ الثِّقَةَ بِكَرَمِكَ حَمَلَتْنِي عَلَى الْجُرْأَةِ عَلَيْكَ، وَإِنَّ الْعَبْدَ إِذَا ضَاقَتْ عَلَيْهِ حِيلَتُهُ قَلَّ حَيَاؤُهُ!

Yā Allāhu bi ayyi rijlin amshī ilayk, am bi ayyi ʿaynin andhuru ilayk, am bi ayyi lisānin unājīk, am bi ayyi yadin adʿūk, lākinith-thiqata bikaramika ḥamalatnī ʿalal-jur'ati ʿalayk, wa innal-ʿabda idhā ḍāqat ʿalayhi ḥīlatuhu qalla ḥayā'uh!

O Allah, with which leg could I walk towards You? With which eye could I look towards You? With which tongue could I converse with You? With which hand could I supplicate to You? But my trust in Your generosity gave me the courage to do so. Truly when the servant has no other option, he loses the sense of shame in his sins![54]

• **32** •

*إِلٰهِي كَيْفَ يُنَاجِيكَ فِي الصَّلَوَاتِ مَنْ يَعْصِيكَ فِي الْخَلَوَاتِ لَوْ لَا حِلْمُكَ،
أَمْ كَيْفَ يَدْعُوكَ فِي الْحَاجَاتِ مَنْ يَنْسَاكَ عِنْدَ الشَّهَوَاتِ لَوْ لَا فَضْلُكَ*

Ilāhī kayfa yunājīka fiṣ-ṣalawāti man yaʿṣīka fil-khalawāti law lā ḥilmuk, am kayfa yadʿūka fil-ḥājāti man yansāka ʿindash-shahawāti law lā faḍluk.

My Lord, if it was not for Your forbearance, how could one who disobeys You in solitude converse with You in prayer? If it was not for Your bounty, how could one who forgets You when engrossed in his desires call out to You when he is in need?[55]

• **33** •

*اَللّٰهُمَّ لَا تَحْرِمْنِي خَيْرَ مَا عِنْدَكَ لِشَرِّ مَا عِنْدِي، اَللّٰهُمَّ لَا تَكِلْنَا إِلَى أَنْفُسِنَا
وَلَا إِلَى النَّاسِ فَنَضِيعُ*

*Allāhumma lā taḥrimnī khayra mā ʿindaka lisharri mā ʿindī,
Allāhumma lā takilnā ilā anfusinā wa lā ilan-nāsi fanaḍīʿ.*

O Allah, do not forbid me the good that You have due to the evil that I have committed. O Allah, do not leave us to ourselves nor to others, otherwise we will be lost.

• 34 •

يَا اللهُ كَمْ مِنْ نِعْمَةٍ أَنْعَمْتَ بِهَا عَلَيَّ قَلَّ لَكَ عِنْدَهَا شُكْرِي، وَكَمْ مِنْ بَلِيَّةٍ اِبْتَلَيْتَنِي بِهَا قَلَّ لَهَا عِنْدَكَ صَبْرِي! يَا مَنْ رَءَانِي عَلَى الْمَعَاصِي فَلَمْ يَفْضَحْنِي، أَعِنِّي عَلَىٰ دِينِي وَدُنْيَايَ

*Yā Allāhu kam min niʿmatin anʿamta bihā ʿalayya qalla laka
ʿindahā shukrī, wa kam min baliyyatin ibtalaytanī bihā qalla
lahā ʿindaka ṣabrī! Yā man raʾānī ʿalal-maʿāṣī falam yafḍaḥnī,
aʿinnī ʿalā dīnī wa dunyāy.*

O Allah, how many blessings have You bestowed upon me for which my gratitude was too little? And how many afflictions did You test me with for which my patience was too little? O One Who sees me when I sin but does not expose me, assist me in my religion and my worldly life.[56]

• 35 •

اَللّٰهُمَّ إِنِّي أَسْأَلُكَ سِتْرَكَ الَّذِي لَا تُزِيلُهُ الرِّيَاحُ وَلَا تَخْرِقُهُ الرِّمَاح

*Allāhumma innī as'aluka sitrakal-ladhī lā tuzīluhur-riyāḥu
wa lā takhriquhur-rimāḥ.*

O Allah, truly I beseech You for Your shield which winds cannot blow away and which spears cannot penetrate.

• 36 •

اَللّٰهُمَّ لَا تُوَلِّنِي غَيْرَكَ، وَلَا تَنْزِعْ عَنِّي سِتْرَكَ، وَلَا تُنْسِنِي ذِكْرَكَ

*Allāhumma lā tuwallinī ghayrak, wa lā tanzi' 'annī sitrak,
wa lā tunsinī dhikrak.*

O Allah, do not entrust me to anyone other than You. Do not expose my sins and do not cause me to neglect Your remembrance.[57]

• 37 •

اَللّٰهُمَّ هَبْنَا عَطَاءَكَ، وَلَا تَكْشِفْ عَنَّا غِطَاءَكَ

Allāhumma habnā ʿaṭāʾak, wa lā takshifʿannā ghiṭāʾak.

O Allah, grant us Your gifts and do not expose our sins by removing from us Your covering.[58]

• 38 •

اَللّٰهُمَّ اسْتُرْنَا عَلَىٰ وَجْهِ الْأَرْضِ، وَارْحَمْنَا فِي بَاطِنِ الْأَرْضِ، وَلَا تَفْضَحْنَا يَوْمَ الْعَرْضِ

Allāhummas-turnā ʿalā wajhil-arḍ, war-ḥamnā fī bāṭinil-arḍ, wa lā tafḍaḥnā yawmal-ʿarḍ.

O Allah, hide our sins whilst we are on the face of the earth, have mercy upon us when we are in the depths of the earth, and do not expose us on the Day of Exposition.

• 39 •

اَللّٰهُمَّ كَمَا عَلَوْتَ بِعَظَمَتِكَ عَلَى الْعُظَمَاءِ، وَانْقَادَ كُلُّ شَيْءٍ لِعَظَمَتِكَ، وَخَضَعَ كُلُّ ذِي سُلْطَانٍ لِسُلْطَانِكَ، وَصَارَ أَمْرُ الدُّنْيَا وَالْآخِرَةِ كُلُّهُ بِيَدِكَ، اِجْعَلْ لِي مِنْ كُلِّ هَمٍّ وَغَمٍّ أَصْبَحْتُ وَأَمْسَيْتُ فِيهِ فَرَجاً وَمَخْرَجاً، إِنَّكَ عَلَى كُلِّ شَيْءٍ قَدِيرٌ. تَتَوَدَّدُ إِلَيَّ بِالنِّعَمِ مَعَ غِنَاكَ عَنِّي، وَأَتَبَغَّضُ إِلَيْكَ بِالْمَعَاصِي مَعَ افْتِقَارِي إِلَيْكَ، فَلَمْ أَرَ مَوْلًى كَرِيماً أَعْطَفَ مِنْكَ عَلَى عَبْدٍ لَئِيمٍ مِثْلِي، يَا رَبِّ مَا تَصْنَعُ بِعَذَابِي وَرَحْمَتُكَ وَسِعَتْ كُلَّ شَيْءٍ، فَلْتَسَعْنِي رَحْمَتُكَ فَإِنِّي لَا شَيْءٍ! وَلَا تُهِنِّي بِذُنُوبِي، وَمَا عَلَيْكَ أَنْ تَعْطِيَنِي الَّذِي أَسْأَلُ، يَا رَبُّ يَا اللهُ يَا أَرْحَمَ الرَّاحِمِينَ

Allāhumma kamā ʿalawta biʿa<u>dh</u>amatika ʿalal-ʿu<u>dh</u>amāʾ, wan-qāda kullu shayʾin liʿa<u>dh</u>amatik, wa khaḍaʿa kullu dhī sulṭānin lisulṭānik, wa ṣāra amrud-dunyā wal-ākhirati kulluhu biyadik, ijʿal lī min kulli hammin wa ghammin aṣbaḥtu wa amsaytu fīhi farajan wa makhrajā, innaka ʿalā kulli shayʾin qadīr. Tatawaddadu ilayya bin-niʿami maʿa ghināka ʿannī, wa atabaghghaḍu ilayka bil-maʿāṣī maʿaf-tiqārī ilayk, falam ara mawlan karīman aʿṭafa minka ʿalā ʿabdin laʾīmin mithlī, yā rabbi mā taṣnaʿu bi ʿadhābī wa raḥmatuka wasiʿat kulla shayʾ, faltasaʿnī raḥmatuka fa ʾinnī lā shayʾ! Wa lā tuhinnī bi dhunūbī, wa mā ʿalayka an taʿṭiyanil-ladhī asʾal yā rabbu yā Allāhu yā arḥamar-rāḥimīn.

O Allah, You are elevated in Your greatness above all those who are great. Everything surrenders to Your greatness, and everyone possessing authority yields to Your authority. All the matters of this world and the next are in Your hands, so make for me a release and a way out from every sorrow and distress that I go through in the day and at night; truly You are capable of all things. You pour Your affection upon me through the bounties You bestow on me, though You have no need of me, and I push them away through my sins, though I am in need of You. I have not seen a generous Lord more compassionate than You to a blameworthy servant like me. O Lord, Your mercy encompasses everything, so let Your mercy accommodate me, for I am nothing! Please do not humiliate me because of my sins. Of course it would not take away from Your bounty, my Lord, if You grant me what I ask. O Lord, O Allah, O Most Merciful of those who show mercy![59]

• 40 •

إِلَهِي كَفَانِي فَخْرًا أَنْ تَكُونَ لِي رَبًّا وَكَفَانِي عِزًّا أَنْ أَكُونَ لَكَ عَبْدًا، أَنْتَ كَمَا أُرِيدُ فَاجْعَلْنِي كَمَا تُرِيدُ

Ilāhī kafānī fakhran an takūna lī rabban wa kafānī ʿizzan an akūna laka ʿabdan, anta kamā urid, fajʿalnī kamā turīd.

My Lord, it is enough esteem for me that You are my Lord, and it is enough honor for me that I am Your servant. You are as I want You to be, so make me as You want me to be.[60]

• 41 •

اَللّٰهُمَّ افْعَلْ بِي وَبِأَهْلِي عَاجِلًا وَآجِلًا فِي الدِّينِ وَالدُّنْيَا وَالدُّنْيَا مَا أَنْتَ لَهُ أَهْلٌ، وَلَا تَفْعَلْ بِنَا يَا مَوْلَانَا مَا نَحْنُ لَهُ أَهْلٌ، إِنَّكَ غَفُورٌ حَلِيمٌ جَوَّادٌ كَرِيمٌ رَؤُوفٌ رَّحِيمٌ

Allāhummaf-ʿal bī wa bi ahlī ʿājilan wa ājilan fid-dīni wad-dunyā mā anta lahu ahl, wa lā tafʿal binā yā mawlānā mā naḥnu lahu ahl, innaka ghafūrun ḥalīmun jawwādun karīmun raʾūfur-raḥīm.

O Allah, treat me and my family in my religious and worldly affairs both now and later in a way that is befitting You, and do not treat us, our Lord, in a way that is befitting us. Truly You are Forgiving, Forbearing, Always Giving, Generous, Tender, and Full of Mercy.[61]

• 42 •

يَا اللهُ يَا مَنْ لَيْسَ مَعَهُ رَبٌّ يُدْعَى، وَيَا مَنْ لَيْسَ فَوْقَهُ خَالِقٌ يُخْشَى، وَيَا مَنْ لَيْسَ لَهُ وَزِيرٌ يُؤْتَى وَلَا حَاجِبٌ يُرْشَى، أَذِقْنَا بَرْدَ عَفْوِكَ وَحَلَاوَةَ مُنَاجَاتِكَ

Yā Allāhu yā man laysa maʿahu rabbun yudʿā, wa yā man laysa fawqahu khāliqun yukhshā, wa yā man laysa lahu wazīrun yuʾtā wa lā ḥājibun yurshā, adhiqnā barda ʿafwika wa ḥalāwata munājātik.

O Allah, O One besides Whom there is no other God to be called upon, O One above Whom there is no creator who is to be feared, O One Who does not have a vizier to be approached instead of Him, nor a doorman to be bribed, allow us to taste the cool relief of Your pardon and the sweetness of intimate discourse with You.

PROTECTION

• 43 •

أَلَيْسَ اللهُ بِكَافٍ عَبْدَهُ

Alaysal-lāhu bi kāfin ‘abdah?

Is not God sufficient for His servant?[62]

• 44 •

حَسْبِيَ اللهُ وَنِعْمَ الْوَكِيلُ، نِعْمَ الْمَوْلَى وَنِعْمَ النَّصِير

Ḥasbiyal-lāhu wa ni‘mal-wakīl, ni‘mal-mawlā wa ni‘man-naṣīr.

Sufficient for me is Allah; the Best Guarantor, the Best Protector, and the Best Helper.[63]

• 45 •

إِنَّ وَلِيِّيَ اللهُ الَّذِي نَزَّلَ الْكِتَابَ وَهُوَ يَتَوَلَّى الصَّالِحِينَ

Inna waliyyiyal-lāhul-ladhī nazzalal-kitāba wa huwa yatawall aṣ-ṣāliḥīn.

Indeed, my guardian is God Who sent down the scripture, and it is He Who takes care of the righteous.[64]

• 46 •

لَا حَوْلَ وَلَا قُوَّةَ إِلَّا بِاللهِ الْعَلِيِّ الْعَظِيمِ

Lā ḥawla wa lā quwwata illā bil-lāhil-ʿaliyyil-ʿadhīm.

There is no power and no strength except with Allah, the Sublime, the Magnificent.[65]

• 47 •

بِسْمِ اللهِ الَّذِي لَا يَضُرُّ مَعَ اسْمِهِ شَيْءٌ فِي الْأَرْضِ وَلَا فِي السَّمَاءِ وَهُوَ السَّمِيعُ الْعَلِيمُ

Bismil-lāhil-ladhī lā yaḍurru maʻasmihi shay'un fil-arḍi wa lā fis-samā'i wa huwas-samīʻul-ʻalīm.

In the name of Allah, by Whose name nothing can cause harm in the earth or in the heavens. He is the One Who hears everything and knows everything.[66]

• 48 •

أَعُوذُ بِكَلِمَاتِ اللهِ التَّامَّاتِ مِنْ شَرِّ مَا خَلَقَ

Aʻūdhu bi kalimātil-lāhit-tāmmāti min sharri mā khalaq.

I seek refuge in the perfect words of Allah from the evil of that which He has created.[67]

• 49 •

أَعُوذُ بِكَلِمَاتِ اللهِ التَّامَّةِ، مِنْ كُلِّ شَيْطَانٍ وَهَامَّةٍ، وَمِنْ كُلِّ عَيْنٍ لَامَّةٍ

Aʿūdhu bi kalimātil-lāhit-tāmmah, min kulli shayṭānin wa hāmmah, wa min kulli ʿaynin lāmmah.

I seek refuge in the perfect words of Allah from every devil, vermin, and evil eye.[68]

• 50 •

اَللّٰهُمَّ إِنِّي أَعُوذُ بِكَ أَنْ أَضِلَّ أَوْ أُضَلَّ، أَوْ أَزِلَّ أَوْ أُزَلَّ، أَوْ أَظْلِمَ أَوْ أُظْلَمَ، أَوْ أَجْهَلَ أَوْ يُجْهَلَ عَلَيَّ

Allāhumma innī aʿūdhu bika an aḍilla aw uḍall, aw azilla aw uzall, aw adhlima aw udhlam aw ajhala aw yujhala ʿalayy.

O Allah, truly I seek refuge in You from going astray or leading others astray, or that I commit an error or that an error is committed against me, or that I behave unjustly or am treated unjustly, or that I should act ignorantly or be treated ignorantly.[69]

• 51 •

ٱللّٰهُمَّ لَا تُشْمِتْ بِي عَدُوِّي وَلَا تَسُوْ بِي صَدِيقِي

Allāhumma lā tushmit bī ʿaduwwī wa lā tasū' bī ṣadīqī.

O Allah, do not allow my enemies to rejoice at my misfortune, and do not allow my friends to be harmed because of me.[70]

• 52 •

ٱللّٰهُمَّ إِنِّي أَعُوذُ بِكَ مِنْ زَوَالِ نِعْمَتِكَ، وَتَحَوُّلِ عَافِيَتِكَ، وَفُجَاءَةِ نِقْمَتِكَ، وَجَمِيع سَخَطِكَ

Allāhumma innī aʿūdhu bika min zawāli niʿmatik, wa taḥawwuli ʿāfiyatik, wa fujā'ati niqmatik, wa jamīʿi sakhaṭik.

O Allah, truly I seek refuge in You from the disappearance of Your blessings, the reversal of the good health You have bestowed on me, the suddenness of Your wrath, and the earning of Your displeasure.[71]

• 53 •

اَللّٰهُمَّ لَا تَجْعَلْنَا مَوْضِعَ شَفَقَةِ عِبَادِكَ وَاجْعَلْنَا دَائِمًا وَأَبَدًا بِكَ وَمَعَكَ وَإِلَيْكَ وَلَا مَنْجَىٰ وَلَا مَلْجَأً مِنْكَ إِلَّا إِلَيْكَ، يَا مَنْ هَجْرُهُ أَعْظَمُ مِنْ نَارِهِ وَوَصْلُهُ أَطْيَبُ مِنْ جَنَّتِهِ يَا أَرْحَمَ الرَّاحِمِينَ

Allāhumma lā taj'alnā mawḍi'a shafaqati 'ibādika waj-'alnā dā'iman wa abadan bika wa ma'aka wa ilayka wa lā manjā wa lā malja'a minka illā ilayk, yā man hajruhu a'<u>dh</u>amu min nārihi wa waṣluhu aṭyabu min jannatihi yā arḥamar-rāḥimīn.

O Allah, do not make us the object of sympathy for Your servants, and make us always and forever travel to You, with You, and through You. There is no refuge and no sanctuary from You except with You. O One from Whom separation is worse than the punishment of His Fire, and with Whom a union is more pleasurable than the attainment of His Paradise, O Most Merciful of those who show mercy.

• 54 •

اَللّٰهُمَّ إِنِّي أَسْأَلُكَ بِنُورِ وَجْهِكَ الَّذِي أَشْرَقَتْ لَهُ السَّمَاوَاتِ وَالْأَرْضِ، أَنْ تَجْعَلَنِي فِي حِرْزِكَ وَحِفْظِكَ وَجِوَارِكَ وَتَحْتَ كَنَفِكَ

Allāhuma innī as'aluka bi nūri wajhikal-ladhī ashraqat lahus-samāwāti wal-arḍ, an taj'alanī fī ḥirzika wa ḥifdhika wa jiwārika wa taḥta kanafik.

O Allah, truly I beseech You by the light of Your countenance, by which the heavens and the earth are illuminated, to place me in Your sanctuary, in Your protection, in Your proximity, and under Your wing.[72]

• 55 •

اَللّٰهُمَّ إِنَّا إِلَيْكَ نَفْزَعُ، وَبَابَكَ نَقْرَعُ، وَلِقُدْرَتِكَ نَخْضَعُ، وَمِنْ عِقَابِكَ نَخْشَعُ، وَبِفَضْلِكَ نُرْوَىٰ وَنَشْبَعُ، وَفِي رِيَاضِكَ نَلْهُو وَنَرْتَعُ

Allāhumma innā ilayka nafza', wa bābaka naqra', wa li qudratika nakhḍagh, wa min 'iqābika nakhsha', wa bi faḍlika nurwā wa nashba', wa fī riyāḍika nalhū wa narta'.

O Allah, truly with You we seek asylum, upon Your door do we knock, to Your power do we surrender, and Your punishment do we dread. By Your bounty we are watered and satiated, and in Your meadows we take pleasure and revel.[73]

• 56 •

اَللّٰهُمَّ إِنِّي أَعُوذُ بِكَ مِنْ شَرِّ نَفْسِي وَشَرِّ الشَّيْطَانِ وَشِرْكِهِ

Allāhumma innī a'ūdhu bika min sharri nafsī wa sharrish-shayṭāni wa shirkih.

O Allah, truly I seek refuge in You from the evil of myself and the evil of Satan and the idolatry he calls to.[74]

• 57 •

اَللّٰهُمَّ إِنِّي أَعُوذُ بِكَ مِنْ أَنْ أَمُوتَ فِي تَطَلُّبِ الدُّنْيَا، اَللّٰهُمَّ زَهِّدْنَا فِي الدُّنْيَا وَوَسِّعْ عَلَيْنَا فِيهَا وَلَا تَزْوِهَا عَنَّا وَلَا تُرَغِّبْنَا فِيهَا

Allāhumma innī a'ūdhu bika min an amūta fī taṭallubid-dunyā, Allāhumma zahhidnā fid-dunyā wa wassi' 'alaynā fīhā wa lā tazwihā 'annā wa lā turaghghibnā fīhā.

O Allah, I seek Your refuge from dying in pursuit of this world. O Allah, help us to be detached from the world, yet increase our sustenance in it; do not push it away from us, but do not make us desirous of it.[75]

• 58 •

اَللّٰهُمَّ إِنِّي أَعُوذُ بِكَ أَنْ أَعْمَلَ عَمَلًا يُخْزَىٰ بِهِ نَبِيِّي وَرَسُولِي وَشَفِيعِي مُحَمَّدٌ صَلَّى اللهُ عَلَيْهِ وَآلِهِ وَسَلَّم

Allāhumma innī a'ūdhu bika an a'mala 'amalan yukhzā bihi nabiyyī wa rasūlī wa shafī'ī Muḥammadun ṣallal-lāhu 'alayhi wa ālihi wa sallam.

O Allah, truly I seek refuge in You that I should do a deed which would shame my Prophet, my Messenger, and my Intercessor, Muḥammad, may the peace and blessings of Allah be upon him and his family.[76]

• 59 •

اَللّٰهُمَّ إِنِّي أَسْأَلُكَ مِنْ خَيْرِ مَا أَحَاطَ بِهِ عِلْمُكَ فِي الدُّنْيَا وَالْآخِرَة، وَأَعُوذُ بِكَ مِنْ شَرِّ مَا أَحَاطَ بِهِ عِلْمُكَ فِي الدُّنْيَا وَالْآخِرَة

Allāhumma innī as'aluka min khayri mā aḥāṭa bihi 'ilmuka fid-dunyā wal-ākhirah, wa a'ūdhu bika min sharri mā aḥāṭa bihi 'ilmuka fid-dunyā wal-ākhirah.

O Allah, truly I beseech You for all the goodness that Your knowledge encompasses in this world and the next, and I seek refuge in You from all the evil that Your knowledge encompasses in this world and the next.[77]

• 60 •

اَللّٰهُمَّ إِنِّي أَعُوذُ بِكَ مِنْ عَذَابِ جَهَنَّمَ، وَأَعُوذُ بِكَ مِنْ عَذَابِ الْقَبْرِ، وَأَعُوذُ بِكَ مِنْ فِتْنَةِ الْمَحْيَا وَالْمَمَاتِ، وَأَعُوذُ بِكَ مِنْ فِتْنَةِ الْمَسِيحِ الدَّجَّالِ

Allāhumma innī aʿūdhu bika min ʿadhābi jahannam, wa aʿūdhu bika min ʿadhābil-qabr, wa aʿūdhu bika min fitnatil-maḥyā wal-mamāt, wa aʿūdhu bika min fitnatil-masīḥid-dajjāl.

O Allah, truly I seek refuge in You from the torment of Hell, and I seek refuge in You from the torment of the grave, and I seek refuge in You from the trials of life and death, and I seek refuge in You from the trials of the Dajjāl (Anti-Christ).[78]

• 61 •

رَبَّنَا آتِنَا فِي الدُّنْيَا حَسَنَةً وَفِي الْآخِرَةِ حَسَنَةً وَقِنَا عَذَابَ النَّارِ

Rabbanā ātinā fid-dunyā ḥasanatan wa fil-ākhirati ḥasanatan wa qinā ʿadhāban-nār.

Our Lord, give us goodness in this world, goodness in the world to come, and save us from the torment of the Fire.[79]

• 62 •

اَللّٰهُمَّ إِنِّي أَسْأَلُكَ الْجَنَّةَ بِلَا عَمَلٍ عَمِلْتُهُ، وَأَعُوذُ بِكَ مِنَ النَّارِ بِلَا ذَنْبٍ تَرَكْتُهُ

Allāhumma innī as'alukal-jannata bilā 'amalin 'amaltuh, wa a'ūdhubika minan-nāri bilā dhambin taraktuh.

O Allah, truly I ask You for Paradise not because of some good I have done, and I seek refuge in You from the Fire not because of some bad I have avoided.[80]

• 63 •

اَللّٰهُمَّ إِنِّي أَسْأَلُكَ الْجَنَّةَ وَمَا قَرَّبَ إِلَيْهَا مِنْ قَوْلٍ وَعَمَلٍ، وَأَعُوذُ بِكَ مِنَ النَّارِ وَمَا قَرَّبَ إِلَيْهَا مِنْ قَوْلٍ وَعَمَلٍ

Allāhumma innī as'alukal-jannata wa mā qarraba ilayhā min qawlin wa 'amal, wa a'ūdhu bika minan-nāri wa mā qarraba ilayhā min qawlin wa 'amal.

O Allah, truly I ask of You Paradise and those words and deeds which will bring me closer to it. I seek refuge in You from the Fire and those words and deeds which will bring me closer to it.[81]

• 64 •

اَللّٰهُمَّ إِنَّكَ أَعْطَيْتَنَا الْإِسْلَامَ مِنْ غَيْرِ أَنْ نَسْأَلَكَ، فَلَا تَحْرِمْنَا الْجَنَّةَ وَنَحْنُ نَسْأَلُكَ

*Allāhumma innaka a'ṭaytanal-islāma min ghayri an nas'alak,
fa lā taḥrimnal-jannata wa naḥnu nas'aluk.*

O Allah, truly You granted us Islam without us having asked
You for it, so do not refuse us Paradise, which we ask You for.

• 65 •

اَللّٰهُمَّ إِنِّي أَسْأَلُكَ الْعَافِيَةَ فِي الدُّنْيَا وَالْآخِرَةِ، اَللّٰهُمَّ إِنِّي أَسْأَلُكَ الْعَفْوَ وَالْعَافِيَةَ فِي دِينِي وَدُنْيَايَ وَأَهْلِي وَمَالِي، اَللّٰهُمَّ اسْتُرْ عَوْرَاتِي وَآمِنْ رَوْعَاتِي، اَللّٰهُمَّ احْفَظْنِي مِنْ بَيْنِ يَدَيَّ وَمِنْ خَلْفِي وَعَنْ يَمِينِي وَعَنْ شِمَالِي وَمِنْ فَوْئِي، وَأَعُوذُ بِعَظَمَتِكَ أَنْ أُغْتَالَ مِنْ تَحْتِي

*Allāhumma innī as'alukal-'āfiyata fid-dunyā wal-ākhirah,
Allāhumma innī as'alukal-'afwa wal-'āfiyata fī dīnī wa
dunyāya wa ahlī wa mālī, Allāhummas-tur 'awrāti wa āmin
raw'ātī, Allāhummaḥ-fadhnī min bayni yadayya wa min
khalfī wa 'an yamīnī wa 'an shimālī wa min fawqī, wa a'ūdhu
bi'adhamatika an ughtāla min taḥtī.*

O Allah, truly I beseech You for well-being in this world
and the next. O Allah, truly I beseech You for pardon and
well-being in my religion, my life, my family, and my wealth.
O Allah, conceal my faults and set my fears at ease. O Allah,
protect me from before me and behind me, from my right
and from my left, and from above me. I seek refuge in Your
magnificence from being seized unawares from below me. [82]

• 66 •

*آللهُ أَكْبَرُ، اللهُ أَعَزُّ مِنْ خَلْقِهِ جَمِيعًا، اللهُ أَعَزُّ مِنْ مَا أَخَافُ وَأَحْذَرُ، أَعُوذُ
بِاللهِ الَّذِي لَا إلهَ إلَّا هُوَ الْمُمْسِكُ السَّمٰوَاتِ السَّبْعَ أَنْ يَقَعْنَ عَلَى الْأَرْضِ إلَّا
بِإِذْنِهِ، مِنْ شَرِّ الظَّالِمِينَ وَجُنُودِهِمْ وَأَتْبَاعِهِمْ وَأَشْيَاعِهِمْ، مِنَ الْجِنَّ وَالْإِنْسِ،
اللّهُمَّ كُنْ لِي جَارًا مِنْ شَرِّهِمْ جَلَّ ثَنَاؤُكَ وَعَزَّ جَارُكَ وَتَبَارَكَ اسْمُكَ وَلَا
إلهَ غَيْرُكَ*

*Allāhu akbar, Allāhu aʻazzu min khalqihi jamīʻā, Allāhu
aʻazzu mimmā akhāfu wa aḥdhar, aʻūdhu bil-lāhil-ladhī lā
ilāha illā huwal-mumsikus-samāwātis-sabʻi an yaqaʻna ʻalal-
arḍi illā biʼithnih, min sharri<u>dh-dh</u>ālimīna wa junūdihim wa
atbāʻihim wa ashyāʻihim, minal-jinni wal-ins, Allāhumma
kun lī jāran min sharrihim jalla thanāʼuka wa ʻazza jāruka
wa tabārakas-muka wa lā ilāha ghayruk.*

Allah is the Greatest, Allah is more powerful than His entire
creation. Allah is more powerful than what we fear and what
we worry about. I seek refuge in Allah, other than Whom

50

there is no god - the One Who holds up all that is in the seven heavens from falling upon us except that of it which He wills - from the evil of the oppressors, their soldiers, their followers, and their adherents among the jinn and among humankind. O Allah, be a shield for me from their evil. Majestic is Your praise, mighty is Your patronage, blessed is Your name, and there is no god but You.[83]

• 67 •

Wa ufawwiḍu amrī ilal-lāh, innal-lāha baṣīrum bil-ʿibād.

I entrust my affairs to Allah. Truly Allah has deep insight into His servants.[84]

Personal Need

• 68 •

أَمَّنْ يُجِيبُ الْمُضْطَرَّ إِذَا دَعَاهُ وَيَكْشِفُ السُّوءَ

Amman yujībul-muḍṭarra idhā daʻāhu wa yakshifus-sū'?

Who else answers the destitute when they call upon Him?
Who is it that removes their troubles?[85]

• 69 •

اَللّٰهُمَّ إِنَّا نَسْأَلُكَ بِاسْمِكَ الْمَخْزُونِ الْمَكْنُونِ الْمُبَارَكِ الطَّيِّبِ الطَّاهِرِ الْمُطَهَّرِ الْمُقَدَّسِ

Allāhumma innā nasʼaluka bis-mikal-makhzūnil-maknūnil-mubārakiṭ-ṭayyibiṭ-ṭāhiril-muṭahharil-muqaddas.

O Allah, truly we beseech You by Your secret, hidden, blessed, good, pure, purified, and holy name.[86]

• 70 •

يَا حَيُّ يَا قَيُّومُ، بِرَحْمَتِكَ أَسْتَغِيثُ

Yā ḥayyu yā qayyūm, bi raḥmatika astaghīth.

O Living, O All-Sustaining, I ask You through Your mercy to help me.[87]

• 71 •

يَا مَنْ كَتَبَ عَلَىٰ نَفْسِهِ الرَّحْمَةَ، ارْحَمْنَا

Yā man kataba ʿalā nafsihir-raḥmah, irḥamnā.

O One Who has prescribed mercy upon Himself, have mercy on us![88]

• 72 •

يَا صَاحِبِي عِنْدَ كُلِّ شِدَّةٍ، وَيَا مُؤْنِسِي عِنْدَ كُلِّ وَحْشَةٍ، يَا ذَا الْجَلَالِ وَالْإِكْرَام

Yā ṣāḥibī 'inda kulli shiddah, wa yā mu'nisī 'inda kulli waḥshah, yā dhal-jalāli wal-ikrām.

O my Companion in every adversity, O Intimate Friend for me in every estrangement,[89] O Possessor of Majesty and Honor.

• 73 •

يَا مُؤْنِسَ كُلِّ وَحِيد، يَا قَرِيباً غَيْرَ بَعِيد، يَا شَاهِداً غَيْرَ غَائِب، يَا غَالِباً غَيْرَ مَغْلُوب، يَا حَيُّ يَا قَيُّوم

Yā mu'nisa kulli waḥīd, yā qarīban ghayra ba'īd, yā shāhidan ghayra ghā'ib, yā ghāliban ghayra maghlūb, yā ḥayyu yā qayyūm.

O Intimate Friend for every lonely person, O One Who is close and not far, O One Who is present and never absent, O One Who vanquishes and is not vanquished, O Living One, O All-Sustaining One.[90]

• 74 •

يَا اللهُ مَا أَضْيَقَ الطَّرِيقَ عَلَى مَنْ لَمْ تَكُنْ دَلِيلَهُ، وَمَا أَوْحَشَ الْبِلَادَ عَلَى مَنْ لَمْ تَكُنْ أَنِيسَهُ

Yā Allāhu mā aḍyaqaṭ-ṭarīqa ʿalā man lam takun dalīlah, wa mā awḥashal-bilāda ʿalā man lam takun anīsah.

O Allah, how constricted is the path for the one who does not have You as his guide, and how lonely are the lands for one who does not have You as his intimate companion.[91]

• 75 •

يَا إِلَهِي مَنْ لِي إِذَا قَطَعْتَنِي وَمَنْ ذَا الَّذِي يَضُرُّنِي إِذَا نَفَعْتَنِي وَمَنْ ذَا الَّذِي يُعَذِّبُنِي إِذَا رَحِمْتَنِي وَمَنْ ذَا الَّذِي يُقَرِّبُنِي إِذَا نَبَذْتَنِي وَمَنْ ذَا الَّذِي يُمْرِضُنِي إِذَا عَافَيْتَنِي

Yā ilāhī man lī idhā qaṭaʿtanī wa man dhal-ladhī yaḍurrunī idhā nafaʿtanī wa man dhal-ladhī yuʿadhdhibunī idhā raḥimtanī wa man dhal-ladhī yuqarribunī idhā nabadhtanī wa man dhal-ladhi yumriḍunī idhā ʿāfaytanī.

O my Lord, who is there for me if You cut me off, and who is it that can harm me if You benefit me? Who is it that can torment me if You have mercy upon me? Who is it that can bring me close if You banish me? Who is it that can make me ill if You bestow upon me good health?[92]

• 76 •

اَللّٰهُمَّ بِكَ نُعَزُّ وَبِغَيْرِكَ نُذَلُّ وَإِيَّاكَ نَرْجُو وَمِنْ غَيْرِكَ نَيْأَسُ

Allāhumma bika nuʿazzu wa bi ghayrika nudhallu wa iyyāka narjū wa min ghayrika nay'as.

O Allah, through You we gain honor and through other than You we are abased. We put all our hopes in You and give up all hope in other than You.[93]

• 77 •

اَللّٰهُمَّ إِنِّي أَسْأَلُكَ يَا مَنْ يَمْلِكُ حَوَائِجَ السَّائِلِينَ، وَيَعْلَمُ ضَمِيرَ الصَّامِتِينَ،
أَسْأَلُكَ بِمَوَاعِيدِكَ الصَّادِقَةِ وَأَيَادِكَ الْفَاضِلَةِ وَرَحْمَتِكَ الْوَاسِعَةِ أَنْ تَفْعَلَ بِي....

Allāhumma innī as'aluka yā man yamliku ḥawā'ijas-sā'ilīn, wa yaʿlamu ḍamīraṣ-ṣāmitīn, as'aluka bimawāʿīdikaṣ-ṣādiqati wa ayādikal-fāḍilati wa raḥmatikal-wāsiʿati an tafʿala bī....

O Allah, truly I beseech You, O One Who possesses that which those who ask are in need of and Who knows the innermost conscience of those who are silent, I beseech You by Your truthful promises, Your generous hands, and Your vast mercy, to *[insert personal request here]*.[94]

• 78 •

يَا رَافِعَ الدَّرَجَاتِ، وَمُنْزِلَ الْبَرَكَاتِ، ضَجَّتْ إِلَيْكَ الْأَصْوَاتُ بِصُنُوفِ اللُّغَاتِ، يَسْأَلُونَكَ الْحَاجَاتِ، فَاعْطِنِي خَيْرَ مَا تُعْطِيَ السَّائِلِينَ يَا ذَا الْجَلَالِ وَالْإِكْرَامِ

Yā rāfi‘ad-darajāt, wa munzilal-barakāt, ḍajjat ilaykal-aṣwātu biṣunūfil-lughāt, yas’alūnakal-ḥājāt, fa‘ṭinī khayra mā tu‘ṭis-sā’ilīna yā dhal-jalāli wal-ikrām.

O Raiser of degrees and Bestower of blessings, voices cry out to You in a variety of languages asking You for their needs, so give me the best of what You give those who ask, O Possessor of Majesty and Honor.

• 79 •

يَا مَوْضِعَ كُلَّ شَكْوَىٰ، وَيَا سَامِعَ كُلَّ نَجْوَىٰ، وَيَا شَاهِدَ كُلَّ بَلْوَىٰ، وَيَا مُنْجِي مُوسَىٰ وَالْمُصْطَفَىٰ، أَدْعُوكَ دُعَاءَ مَنِ اشْتَدَّتْ فَاقَتُهُ وَضَعُفَتْ حَرَكَتُهُ وَقَلَّتْ حِيلَتُهُ، دُعَاءَ الْغَرِيبِ الْغَرِيقِ الْفَقِيرِ الَّذِي لَا يَجِدُ لِكَشْفِ مَا هُوَ فِيهِ إِلَّا أَنْتَ يَا أَرْحَمَ الرَّاحِمِين، لَا إِلٰهَ إِلَّا أَنْتَ إِنِّي كُنْتُ مِنَ الظَّالِمِين

Yā mawḍi‘a kulla shakwā, wa yā sāmi‘a kulla najwā, wa yā shāhida kulla balwā, wa yā munjī Mūsā wal-Muṣṭafā, ad‘ūka du‘ā’a manish-taddat fāqatuhu wa ḍa‘ufat ḥarakatuhu wa qallat ḥīlatuh, du‘ā’al-gharībil-gharīqil-faqīril-ladhī lā yajidu likashfi mā huwa fīhi illā anta yā arḥamar-rāḥimīn, lā ilāha illā anta innī kuntu mina<u>dh</u>-<u>dh</u>ālimīn.

O Receiver of every complaint, O Hearer of every secret conversation, O One Who witnesses every affliction, O Savior of Moses and the Chosen One (Muḥammad ﷺ), I call upon You with the supplication of one whose poverty has intensified, whose ability to move has weakened, and whose attempts have all failed. I call upon You with the supplication of a poor, drowning stranger who finds no one but You to remove the difficulties he is going through, O Most Merciful of those who show mercy. There is no god but You; truly I have been of those who do wrong.[95]

• 80 •

يَا مُجِيبُ يَا مُغِيثُ، مَا طَابَتِ الدُّنْيَا إِلَّا بِذِكْرِكَ وَمَعْرِفَتِكَ، وَلَا الْآخِرَةُ إِلَّا بِقُرْبِكَ وَرُؤْيَتِكَ، حَاشَا أَنْ نَقْنَطَ مِنْ جُودِكَ، فَضْلُكَ جَزِيلٌ وَكَرَمُكَ جَلِيلٌ

*Yā mujību yā mughīthu mā ṭābatid-dunyā illā bidhikrika wa
ma'rifatik, wa lal-ākhiratu illā biqurbika wa ru'yatik, ḥāshā
an naqnaṭa min jūdik, faḍluka jazīlun wa karamuka jalīl.*

O One Who responds to those who call upon Him, O
Deliverer from distress, the world is not made pleasant
except by remembrance of You and knowledge of You.
Likewise, the next world is not made pleasant except by
nearness to You and gazing upon You. Far be it from us to
despair of Your generosity; Your bounty is abundant, Your
generosity is great.

• 81 •

اللّٰهُمَّ إِنِّي أَسْأَلُكَ الْفَوْزَ عِنْدَ الْقَضَاءِ، وَمَنَازِلَ الشُّهَدَاءِ، وَعَيْشَ السُّعَدَاءِ، وَالنَّصْرَ عَلَى الْأَعْدَاءِ، وَمُرَافَقَةَ الْأَنْبِيَاءِ

Allāhumma innī as'alukal-fawza 'indal-qaḍā', wa manāzilash-shuhadā', wa 'ayshas-su'adā', wan-naṣra 'alal-a'dā', wa murāfaqat al-ambiyā'.

O Allah, truly I ask You to make me successful by whole-heartedly accepting whatever You decree. I ask You for the rank of the martyrs and the life of those who are eternally blissful. I ask of You victory over my enemies and the close companionship of the prophets.[96]

• 82 •

اَللّٰهُمَّ اجْعَلِ الْإِسْلَامَ مُنْتَهَى رِضَايَ وَخُذْ إِلَى الْخَيْرِ بِنَاصِيَتِي يَا ذَا الْجَلَالِ وَالْإِكْرَامِ

Allāhummaj-'alil-islāma muntahā riḍāya wa khudh ilal-khayri bi nāṣiyatī yā dhal-jalāli wal-ikrām.

O Allah, make Islam the pinnacle of my pleasure. Take me by my forelock toward goodness, O Possessor of Majesty and Honor.[97]

• 83 •

اَللّٰهُمَّ إِنِّي عَبْدُكَ وَابْنُ عَبْدِكَ وَابْنُ أَمَتِكَ، نَاصِيَتِي بِيَدِكَ، مَاضٍ فِيَّ حُكْمُكَ، عَدْلٌ فِيَّ قَضَاؤُكَ، أَسْأَلُكَ بِكُلِّ اسْمٍ سَمَّيْتَ بِهِ نَفْسَكَ أَوْ أَنْزَلْتَهُ فِي كِتَابِكَ، أَوْ عَلَّمْتَهُ أَحَدًا مِنْ خَلْقِكَ، أَوِ اسْتَأْثَرْتَ بِهِ فِي عِلْمِ الْغَيْبِ عِنْدَكَ، أَنْ تَجْعَلَ الْقُرْآنَ الْعَظِيمَ رَبِيعَ قَلْبِي وَنُورَ صَدْرِي وَجَلَاءَ حُزْئِ وَذَهَابَ هَمِّي

Allāhumma innī ʿabduka wab-nu ʿabdika wab-nu amatik, nāṣiyatī bi yadik, māḍin fiyya ḥukmuk, ʿadlun fiyya qaḍāʾuk, asʾaluka bi kullis-min sammayta bihi nafsaka aw anzaltahu fī kitābik, aw ʿallamtahu aḥadan min khalqik, awis-taʾtharta bihi fī ʿilmil-ghaybi ʿindak, an tajʿalal-qurʾānal-ʿadhīma rabīʿa qalbī wa nūra ṣadrī wa jalāʾa ḥuznī wa dhahāba hammī.

O Allah, truly I am Your servant, the child of Your servant and the child of Your maid-servant. You hold me by my forelock; what You have decreed for me must be, and what You have pre-ordained is just. I beseech You by every name of Yours which You have named Yourself, or have revealed in Your book, or which You have taught to any of Your creation, or which You have kept known only to Yourself, that You make the glorious Qurʾān the spring of my heart, the light of my breast, the departure of my sorrow, and the parting of my distress.[98]

• 84 •

اَللّٰهُمَّ أَعِنِّي عَلَىٰ ذِكْرِكَ وَشُكْرِكَ وَحُسْنِ عِبَادَتِكَ

Allāhumma a'innī 'alā dhikrika wa shukrika wa ḥusni 'ibādatik.

O Allah, assist me in remembering You, thanking You, and worshipping You in an excellent manner.[99]

• 85 •

اَللّٰهُمَّ يَا مُقَلِّبَ الْقُلُوبِ ثَبِّتْ قَلْبِي عَلَىٰ دِينِكَ

Allāhumma yā muqallibal-qulūbi thabbit qalbī 'alā dīnik.

O Allah, O Turner of hearts, make firm my heart upon Your religion.[100]

• 86 •

اَللّٰهُمَّ اكْفِنِي بِحَلَالِكَ عَنْ حَرَامِكَ وَأَغْنِنِي بِفَضْلِكَ عَمَّنْ سِوَاكَ

Allāhummak-finī bi ḥalālika 'an ḥarāmika wa aghninī bi faḍlika 'amman siwāk.

O Allah, suffice me with what is lawful so that I do not go seeking the unlawful, and enrich me with Your bounty so that I do not turn to anyone besides You.[101]

• 87 •

اَللّٰهُمَّ أَصْلِحْ لِي شَأْنِي كُلَّهُ، وَلَا تَكِلْنِي إِلَى نَفْسِي طَرْفَةَ عَيْنٍ

Allāhumma aṣliḥ lī sha'nī kullah, wa lā takilnī ilā nafsī ṭarfata ʿayn.

O Allah, set right my entire state of affairs and do not leave me to myself even for the blink of an eye.[102]

• 88 •

سُبْحَانَ مَنْ لَا يُخَيِّبُ مَنْ قَصَدَهُ، فَاللّٰهُمَّ أَشْغِلْنَا بِذِكْرِكَ عَمَّنْ سِوَاكَ وَاكْشِفْ عَنَّا الْحُجُبَ حَتَّىٰ نَرَاكَ

Subḥāna man lā yukhayyibu man qaṣadah, fal-lāhumma ashghilnā bi dhikrika ʿamman siwāka wak-shif ʿannal-ḥujuba ḥattā narāk.

Glory to the One Who does not disappoint the one who seeks Him. We ask You, O Allah, to preoccupy us in Your

remembrance and lift from us the veils so that we behold
You.

• 89 •

ٱلْحَمْدُ لِلّهِ الَّذِي لَا يُخَيِّبُ مَنْ دَعَاهُ، الْحَمْدُ لِلّهِ الَّذِي هُوَ ثِقَتُنَا حِينَ تَنْقَطِعُ عَنَّا الْحِيَلُ

*Alḥamdu lil-lāhil-ladhī lā yukhayyibu man da'āh, alḥamdu
lil-lāhil-ladhī huwa thiqatunā ḥīna tanqaṭi'u 'annal-ḥiyal.*

Praise be to Allah Who does not disappoint whoever calls
upon Him. Praise be to Allah Who is our reliance when all
our faculties have been exhausted.[103]

ṢALAWĀT

(Lauding the Prophet ﷺ)

• 90 •

اَللّٰهُمَّ صَلِّ عَلَىٰ سَيِّدِنَا مُحَمَّدٍ صَلَاةً تُخْرِجُنَا بِهَا يَا اللهُ مِنْ ظُلُمَاتِ الْوَهْمِ وَتُكْرِمُنَا بِهَا بِنُورِ الْفَهْمِ، وَتَهَبُ لَنَا بِهَا أَكْمَلَ الْمُرَادِ فِي دَارِ الدُّنْيَا وَالْمَعَادِ

Allāhumma ṣalli ‘alā sayyidinā Muḥammad, ṣalātan tukhrijunā bihā yā Allāhu min <u>dh</u>ulumātil-wahmi wa tukrimunā bihā binūril-fahmi wa tahabu lanā bihā akmalal-murādi fī dārid-dunyā wal-ma‘ād.

O Allah, bless Sayyidinā Muhammad a blessing through which You remove us from the darkness of delusion, and through which You honor us with the light of understanding, and through which You grant us everything we wish for in this life and the next.

• 91 •

اَللّٰهُمَّ صَلِّ عَلَىٰ سَيِّدِنَا مُحَمَّدٍ، طِبِّ الْقُلُوبِ وَدَوَائِهَا، وَعَافِيَةِ الْأَبْدَانِ وَشِفَائِهَا، وَنُورِ الْأَبْصَارِ وَضِيَائِهَا، وَعَلَىٰ آلِهِ وَصَحْبِهِ وَسَلِّمْ

Allāhumma ṣalli ‘alā sayyidinā Muḥammad, ṭibbil-qulūbi wa dawā’ihā, wa ‘āfiyatil-abdāni wa shifā’ihā, wa nūril-abṣāri wa ḍiyā’ihā, wa ‘alā ālihi wa ṣaḥbihi wa sallim.

O Allah, bless Sayyidinā Muhammad, the medicine of our hearts and their cure, the health of our bodies and their healing, and the light of our eyes and their illumination.[104]

Between the Desirer and the Desired

طُوبَىٰ لِمَنْ وَصَلَكَ بِحُبِّهِ وَالِهًا

وَسَهِرَ لَيْلَهُ يَتَقَلَّبُ سَاجِدًا دَاعِيًا

كَيْفَ يُرْوَىٰ الظَّمْآنُ مِنْ بَحْرِ جُودِكَ

أَوْ يَتَعَرَّضُ لِنَفَحَاتِكَ مَنْ بَاتَ عَاصِيًا

لَوْ يَعْلَمِ الْأَنَامُ مَا ادَّخَرْتَ لَهُمْ

لَأَتَوْكَ حَبْوًا وَلَا اكْتَحَلَ بِالنَّوْمِ لَاهِيًا

أَتُوبُ مِنَ الذَّنْبِ ثُمَّ أَطْرُقُ بَابَهُ ثَانِيَةً

لَسْتُ بِمُسْتَهْزِئٍ وَلٰكِنْ صَارَ الْقَلْبُ قَاسِيًا

كَذَبَ مَنِ ادَّعَىٰ حُبَّكَ وَهُوَ لَا يَهْوَاكَ

وَإِلَّا لَاسْتَعَارَ لِلْفَقْرِ جِلْبَابًا كَاسِيَا

عَجِبْتُ لِنَفْسٍ لَا يَسْتَقِيمُ اعْوِجَاجُهَا

فَتَاهَتْ عَنْ أُنْسِكَ فَأَمْسَتْ نَسْيًا مَنْسِيَّا

كَيْفَ السَّبِيلُ بِأَنْ أُقِيمَ بِفِنَائِكَ

فَالْقَلْبُ مَشْغُوفٌ يُهَمْهِمُ بِالضَّرَاعَةِ بَاكِيَا

مَا زَالَ أَهْلُ الزَّيْغِ يُرِيدُونَ أَسْرِي

وَعُبَيْدُكَ يُهَرْوِلُ إِلَيْكَ لِفَكِّ رَقَبَتِهِ جَارِيَا

حِلْمُكَ عَلَى الظَّالِمِينَ قَدْ أَضَرَّ بِمَظْلُومٍ

يَلْهَفُ لِرُؤْيَةِ دِينِكَ يَعْلُو عَالِيَا

لِئَامُ بَنِي جِلْدَتِنَا رَغِبُوا عَنْكَ إِلَى هُبَلِ

فَأَعِزَّ دَوْلَتَكَ يَا مُغِيثُ وَكُنْ لَنَا وَالِيَا

رَأَيْتُ النَّاسَ يَطْلُبُونَ الْجَنَّةَ، وَأَنَا

أَعْشَقُ رَبَّهَا فَالْجَارُ قَبْلَ الدَّارِ لِأَنْعَمَ هَانِيَا

بِحَقِّ أَحْمَدٍ عَلَيْكَ إِلَّا سَتَرْتَ عِرْضِي

وَلَا تَفْضَحْنِي بَيْنَ خَلْقِكَ فَأَنْكَشِفُ عَارِيَا

مَا أَعْظَمَ نَعِيمِ الْمُحِبِّ إِذَا لَقِيَ مَحْبُوبَهُ

بَعْدَ طُولِ شَوْقٍ فَخُذْنِي إِلَيْكَ رَاضِيًا

Ṭūbā liman waṣalaka biḥubbihi wālihā

Wasahira laylahu yataqallabu sājidan dāʿiyā

Kayfa yurwaḍ-ḍamʾānu min baḥri jūdik

Aw yataʿarraḍu linafaḥātika man bāta ʿāṣiyā

Law yaʿlamil-anāmu mad-dakharta lahum

Laʿatawka ḥabwan wa lak-taḥala bin-nawmi lāhiyā

Atūbu minadh-dhanbi thumma aṭruqu bābahu thāniyah

Lastu bimustahziʾin wa lākin ṣāral-qalbu qāsiyā

Kadhaba manid-daʿā ḥubbaka wa huwa lā yahwāk

Wa illā las-taʿāra lil-faqri jilbāban kāsiyā

ʿAjibtu linafsin lā yastaqīmuʿ-wijājahā

Fatāhat ʿan unsika faʾamsat nasyan mansiyyā

Kayfas-sabīlu biʾan uqīma bifināʾik

Fal-qalbu mashghūfun yuhamhimu biḍ-ḍarāʿati bākiyā

Mā zāla ahluz-zayghi yurīdūna asrī

Waʻubayduka yuharwilu ilayka lifakki raqabatihi jāriyā

Ḥilmuka ʻala<u>dh</u>-<u>dh</u>ālimīna qad aḍarra bima<u>dh</u>lūm

Yalhafu liruʼyati dīnika yaʻlū ʻāliyā

Liʼāmu banī jildatinā raghibū ʻanka ilā hubal

Faʼaʻizzu dawlataka yā mughīthu wa kun lanā wāliyā

Raʼaytun-nāsa yaṭlubūnal-jannata wa ana

Aʻshaqu rabbahā fal-jāru qablad-dāri liʼanʻama hāniyā

Biḥaqqi aḥmadin ʻalayka illā satarta ʻirḍī

Walā tafḍaḥnī bayna khalqika faʼankashifu ʻāriyā

Mā aʻ<u>dh</u>ama naʻīmil-muḥibbi idhā laqiya maḥbūbahu

Baʻda ṭūli shawqin fakhudhnī ilayka rāḍiyā

Glad tidings to the one who reaches You
by way of wild affection,

Who spends his night alternating between
prostration and supplication.

How can the one who is thirsty for You ever receive his
fill from the ocean of Your generous givings?

Or how can the one who spends his night in disobedience be exposed to Your breezes of blessings?

If only humankind knew what You have in store
for them of treasure,

They would come to You crawling, undistracted
by sleep's pleasure.

I repent from my sin, then again I find myself knocking
upon its door

Not out of mockery, my Lord!
My heart's softness please restore!

He lies who claims to love You but is not
devoted to You,

Or else he would have detached himself
from everything besides You.

I wonder at the soul which does not
straighten up its crookedness,

It wanders away from Your intimacy and becomes
lost in nothingness.[105]

For me to reside at Your front door,
tell me what is the way?

The heart is lost in love,
weeping and mumbling away.

The people of deviation are still trying
to capture me,

And Your servant is hastening toward You
to set himself free.

Your forbearance of the oppressors
pains the oppressed

Who yearn to see Your religion rise
in glory above the rest.

Depraved are they who prefer idols
over You and transgress,

Strengthen Your nation and be our Guardian,
O Deliverer from distress!

I see the people seeking Paradise,
whereas I seek its Lord

For happiness is found in the neighbor,
not the abode.

By the right of Ahmad upon You,
cover me and protect my dignity,

Do not disgrace me, with my faults bared
for all to see.

Oh, the bliss of the lover when he meets his beloved after
the pain of his yearning is eased!

So take me to You when You are satisfied with
me and well-pleased.

Murād Mujāhid al-Ashʿarī al-ʿAdnānī

Afterword

The following supplications are a special gift to the reader. They are prayers that are well-known and helpful for group worship activities and individual practice. You will hear them recited at many Rabata events.

SOME SUPPLICATIONS THAT CAN BE
SAID AFTER OBLIGATORY PRAYERS

• 1 •

اللّٰهُم أَنْتَ السَّلَامُ، وَمِنْكَ السَّلَامُ، وَإِلَيْكَ يَعُودُ السَّلَام، فَحَيِّنَا رَبَّنَا بِالسَّلَام، وَأَدْخِلْنَا الْجَنَّةَ دَارَ السَّلَامِ بِسَلَامٍ، تَبَارَكْتَ وَتَعَالَيْتَ يَا ذَا الْجَلَالِ وَالْإِكْرَام.

Allāhumma antas-salām, wa minkas-salām, wa ilayka ya'ūdus-salām, faḥayyinā rabbanā bis-salām, wa adkhilnal-jannata dāras-salāmi bisalām, tabārakta wa ta'ālayta yā dhal-jalāli wal-ikrām.

O God, You are Peace, and from You is Peace, and to You returns Peace, so greet us, O Lord, with Peace, and enter us into Paradise, the home of peace, in peace. You are the exalted and elevated, O Lord of Majesty and Honor.

• 2 •

اللَّهُمَّ أَعِنَّا عَلَى دَوَامِ ذِكْرِكَ وَشُكْرِكَ وَحُسْنِ عِبَادَتِكَ، وَلَا تَجْعَلْنَا مِنَ الْغَافِلِينَ عَنْ ذِكْرِكَ وَلَا عَنْ شُكْرِكَ وَلَا عَنْ طَاعَتِكَ.

Allāhumma a'innā 'alā dawāmi dhikrika wa shukrika wa ḥusni 'ibādatik, wa lā taj'alnā minal-ghāfilīna 'an dhikrika wa lā 'an shukrika wa lā 'an ṭā'atik.

O Lord, assist us in the constant remembrance and thanking of You, and aid us in our unremitting worship of You. Do not make us of those who are negligent in remembering You, or those who overlook thanking You, and keep us, O Lord, in constant obedience to You.

• 3 •

اللَّهُمَّ أَرِنَا الْحَقَّ حَقًّا وَارْزُقْنَا اتِّبَاعَهُ، وَأَرِنَا الْبَاطِلَ بَاطِلًا وَارْزُقْنَا اجْتِنَابَهُ، وَلَا تَجْعَلْهُمَا عَلَيْنَا مُتَشَابِهَيْنِ فَنَتَّبِعَ الْهَوَىٰ فَنَضِلَّ.

Allāhumma arinal-ḥaqqa ḥaqqan warzuqnat-tibā'ah, wa arinal-bāṭila bāṭilan warzuqnaj-tinābah, wa lā taj'alhumā 'alaynā mutashābihayni fanattabi'al-hawā fanaḍill.

O Lord, show us what is right as right, and grant us the ability to follow that which is right, and show us what is wrong as wrong, and grant us the ability to avoid that which is wrong, and do not make the two alike in our eyes so that we follow our own desires and thus go astray.

• 4 •

اللَّهُمَّ إِنَّا نَسْأَلُكَ عِيْشَةً هَنِيئَةً، وَمِيتَةً سَوِيَّةً، وَحُسْنَ الْخِتَامِ، وَالْوَفَاةَ عَلَى الْإِيْمَانِ مِنْ غَيْرِ مِحْنَةٍ.

Allāhumma innā nas'aluka 'īshatan hanī'ah, wa mītatan sawiyyah, wa ḥusnal-khitām, wal-wafāta 'alal-īmāni min ghayri miḥnah.

O Allah, we ask You for a fulfilled life, a smooth death, a virtuous end, and that we die upon faith without trial.

77

• 5 •

إِلَى شَرَفِ النَّبِيِّ وَآلِهِ وَعَلَى نِيَّةِ الْقُبُولِ والْفُتُوحِ، والْمَغْفِرةِ وَالرَّحْمَةِ، ونَصْرِ دِينِ الْإِسْلَامِ، الْفَاتِحَة.

Ilā sharafin-nabiyyi wa 'ālihi wa 'alā niyyatil-qubūl, wal-futūḥ, wal-maghfirah, war-raḥmah, wa naṣri dīnil-islām, al-Fātiḥa (recite Sūrat al-Fātiḥa here).

For the honor of the Prophet ﷺ and his kin, and with the intention of acceptance and opening, forgiveness and mercy, and the victory of Islam, *al-Fātiḥa* (recite Sūrat al-Fātiḥa here).

Supplications That Can Be Said After Each Two Rak'ahs of Tarāwīḥ Prayer in Ramaḍān

• 6 •

اللَّهُمَّ إِنَّا نَعُوذُ بِرِضَاكَ مِنْ سَخَطِكَ، وَبِمُعَافَاتِكَ مِنْ عُقُوبَتِكَ، وَبِكَ مِنْكَ لَا نُحْصِي ثَنَاءً عَلَيْكَ أَنْتَ كَمَا أَثْنَيْتَ عَلَى نَفْسِكَ.

Allāhumma innā na'ūdhu biriḍāka min sakhaṭik, wa bimu'āfātika min 'uqūbatik, wa bika minka lā nuḥṣī thanā'an 'alayka anta kamā athnayta 'alā nafsik.

O Allah, we seek refuge in Your good pleasure from Your wrath, and we seek refuge in Your pardon from Your punishment, and we seek refuge in You from You. We cannot truly praise You as You deserve to be praised; You are as You have praised Yourself. [106]

A Version of Du‘ā’ al-Qunūt

• 7 •

اَللَّهُمَّ اهْدِنَا فِيمَنْ هَدَيْتَ، وَعَافِنَا فِيمَنْ عَافَيْتَ، وَتَوَلَّنَا فِيمَنْ تَوَلَّيْتَ، وَبَارِكْ لَنَا فِيمَا أَعْطَيْتَ، وَقِنَا شَرَّ مَا قَدَّرْتَ وَقَضَيْتَ، فَإِنَّكَ تَقْضِي وَلَا يُقْضَى عَلَيْكَ، وَإِنَّهُ لَا يَذِلُّ مَنْ وَالَيْتَ، وَلَا يَعِزُّ مَنْ عَادَيْتَ، تَبَارَكْتَ رَبَّنَا وَتَعَالَيْتَ، لَكَ الْحَمْدُ عَلَى مَا قَضَيْتَ، وَلَكَ الشُّكْرُ عَلَى مَا أَعْطَيْتَ، نَسْتَغْفِرُكَ وَنَتُوبُ إِلَيْكَ، اللَّهُمَّ يَا وَاصِلَ الْمُنْقَطِعِينَ أَوْصِلْنَا إِلَيْكَ، وَأَحْسِنْ وُقُوفَنَا بَيْنَ يَدَيْكَ، وَلَا تُخْزِنَا يَوْمَ الْعَرْضِ عَلَيْكَ، وَصَلَّى اللهُ عَلَى سَيِّدِنَا مُحَمَّدٍ وَعَلَى آلِهِ وَصَحْبِهِ وَسَلَّم.

Allāhummah-dinā fī man hadayt, wa ‘āfinā fī man ‘āfayt, wa tawallanā fī man tawallayt, wa bārik lanā fī mā a‘ṭayt, wa qinā sharra mā qaddarta wa qaḍayt, fa’innaka taqḍī wa lā yuqḍā ‘alayk, wa’innahu lā yadhillu man wālayt, wa lā ya‘izzu man ‘ādayt, tabārakta rabbanā wa ta‘ālayt, lakal-ḥamdu ‘alā mā qaḍayt, wa lakash-shukru ‘alā mā a‘ṭayt, nastagh-firuka wa natūbu ilayk, allāhumma yā wāṣilal-munqaṭi‘īna awṣilnā ilayk, wa aḥsin wuqūfanā bayna yadayk, wa lā tukhzinā yawmal-‘arḍi ‘alayk, wa ṣallal-lāhu ‘alā sayyidinā muḥammadin wa ‘alā ālihi wa ṣaḥbihi wa sallam.

O Allah! Guide us among those You guide, grant us health and pardon among those You grant health and pardon, look after us among those You look after, bless us in what

You have bestowed upon us, and protect us from the evil of what You have ordained; for You decree and none decrees against You. None is abased whom You befriend, and none is exalted whom You are at enmity with. O our Lord Who is above all things sacred and exalted, all praise is Yours for what You decree, and all gratitude is due to You for what You have bestowed. We ask Your forgiveness and turn to You in repentance. O Allah, O He Who establishes a connection with those who are cut off, connect us to You, make excellent our standing before You, and do not disgrace us on the day when our deeds are presented before You. O Allah, send your peace and blessings upon Sayyidinā Muḥammad, his family, and his companions.

Some supplications that can be said after Ṣalāt al-Ḥājah

(the Prayer of Need)

• 8 •

لَا إِلَهَ إِلَّا اللهُ الْحَلِيمُ الْكَرِيمُ، سُبْحَانَ اللهِ رَبِّ الْعَرْشِ الْعَظِيمِ، الْحَمْدُ لِلهِ رَبِّ الْعَالَمِينِ، أَسْأَلُكَ مُوجِبَاتِ رَحْمَتِكَ، وَعَزَائِمَ مَغْفِرَتِكَ وَالْغَنِيمَةَ مِنْ كُلِّ بِرٍّ، وَالسَّلَامَةَ مِنْ كُلِّ إِثْمٍ، لَا تَدَعْ لِي ذَنْبًا إِلَّا غَفَرْتَهُ، وَلَا هَمًّا إِلَّا فَرَّجْتَهُ، وَلَا حَاجَةً هِيَ لَكَ رِضًا إِلَّا قَضَيْتَهَا يَا أَرْحَمَ الرَّاحِمِينَ.

*Lā ilāha illal-lāhul-ḥalīmul-karīm, subḥānal-lāhi rabbil-
'arshil-'adhim, al-ḥamdu lil-lāhi rabbil- 'ālamīn, as'aluka
mūjibāti raḥmatika wa 'azā'ima maghfiratik, wal-ghanīmata
min kulli birr, was-salāmata min kulli ithm, lā tada' lī
dhamban illā ghafartah, wa lā hamman illā farrajtah, wa lā
hājatan hiya laka riḍan illā qaḍaytahā yā arḥamar-rāḥimīn.*

There is no God but Allah, the Forbearing and Generous, Glory be to Allah, Lord of the Magnificent Throne; all praise is to Allah, Lord of the worlds. I implore You for everything that causes Your mercy to descend, and for Your certain forgiveness, and for enrichment in every goodness, and for security from committing sins. Leave not a sin of mine except that You forgive it, nor any concern except that You create for it a way out, nor any need in which there is Your good pleasure except that You fulfill it, O Most Merciful of those who show mercy!

• 9 •

لَا إِلَهَ إِلَّا اللهُ الْعَظِيمُ الْحَلِيمُ، لَا إِلَهَ إِلَّا اللهُ رَبُّ السَّمَاوَاتِ وَرَبُّ الْأَرْضِ، رَبُّ الْعَرْشِ الْعَظِيمِ

Lā ilāha illal-lāhul-ʿaḍhīmul-ḥalīm, lā ilāha illal-lāhu rabbus-samāwāti wa rabbul-arḍ, rabbul-ʿarshil- ʿaḍhīm

There is no God but Allah, the Magnificent and Forbearing, there is no God but Allah, Lord of the heavens and the earth, Lord of the Magnificent Throne.[107]

• 10 •

الله ُ الله ُ رَبِّى لَا أُشْرِكُ بِهِ شَيْئًا

Allāhu Allāhu rabbī lā ushriku bihi shay'ā

Allah, Allah is my Lord, I associate nothing with Him.[108]

Du‘ā’ for Ṣalāt al-Istikhārah
(the Prayer for Guidance)

• 11 •

اللَّهُمَّ إِنِّي أَسْتَخِيرُكَ بِعِلْمِكَ، وَأَسْتَقْدِرُكَ بِقُدْرَتِكَ، وَأَسْأَلُكَ مِنْ فَضْلِكَ الْعَظِيمِ، فَإِنَّكَ تَقْدِرُ وَلَا أَقْدِرُ، وَتَعْلَمُ وَلَا أَعْلَمُ، وَأَنْتَ عَلَّامُ الْغُيُوبِ، اللَّهُمَّ إِنْ كُنْتَ تَعْلَمُ أَنَّ هَذَا الْأَمْرَ خَيْرٌ لِي فِي دِينِي وَمَعَاشِي وَعَاقِبَةِ أَمْرِي فَاقْدُرْهُ لِي وَيَسِّرْهُ لِي ثُمَّ بَارِكْ لِي فِيهِ، وَإِنْ كُنْتَ تَعْلَمُ أَنَّ هَذَا الْأَمْرَ شَرٌّ لِي فِي دِينِي وَمَعَاشِي وَعَاقِبَةِ أَمْرِي فَاصْرِفْهُ عَنِّي، وَاصْرِفْنِي عَنْهُ، وَاقْدُرْ لِيَ الْخَيْرَ حَيْثُ كَانَ ثُمَّ أَرْضِنِي بِهِ.

Allāhumma innī astakhīruka bi‘ilmik, wa astaqdiruka biqudratik, wa as’aluka min faḍlikal-‘adhīm, fa’innaka taqdiru wa lā aqdiru, wa ta‘lamu wa lā a‘lamu, wa anta ‘allāmul-ghuyūb. Allāhumma in kunta ta‘lamu anna hādhal-amra [insert matter here] khayrun lī fī dīnī wa ma‘āshī wa ‘āqibati amrī faq-durhu lī wa yassirhu lī thumma bārik lī fīh, wa in kunta ta‘lamu anna hādhal-amra sharrun lī fī dīnī

*wa ma'āshī wa'āqibati amrī faṣ-rifhu 'annī waṣ-rifnī 'anhu,
waq-dur liyal-khayra ḥaythu kāna thumma ar-ḍinī bih.*

O Allah, I seek from You what is best in Your knowledge, and I seek from You strength through Your power, and I ask You from Your immense bounty. For truly You are capable and I am not, You know and I know not, and You are the Knower of the unseen. O Allah, if You know that this matter [insert matter here] is good for me with regard to my religion, my livelihood, and my hereafter, then ordain it for me and facilitate it for me, and grant me blessing in it. And if You know that this matter is harmful for me with regard to my religion, my livelihood, and my hereafter, then turn it away from me and turn me away from it, and ordain for me whatever is better for me wherever it may be, and make me content with it. [109]

Tasbīḥ for Ṣalāt at-Tasābīḥ

• 12 •

سُبْحَانَ اللهِ، وَالْحَمْدُ لِلّهِ، وَلَا إِلهَ إِلَّا اللهُ، وَاللهُ أَكْبَرُ

*Subḥānal-lāh, wal-ḥamdu lil-lāh, wa lā ilāha illal-lāh,
wal-lāhu akbar.*

Glory be to Allah, praise be to Allah, there is no god but
Allah, and Allah is the Greatest.[110]

How to pray Ṣalāt at-Tasābīḥ: The prayer of praise
is prayed like any other prayer but with the addi-
tion of the above phrases of praise. The entire series
is repeated 10 times in each movement of the prayer
and 15 times in the first standing of each rak‘ah. You
can find more information and watch a demonstration
video on this prayer at this link: bit.ly/prayerofpraise.

SEVEN ADHKĀR

• 1 •

لَا حَوْلَ وَلَا قُوَّةَ إِلَّا بِاللهِ الْعَلِيِّ الْعَظِيم

Lā ḥawla wa lā quwwata illā bil-lāhil-'aliyyil-'a<u>dh</u>īm

There is no power and no strength except in Allah, the
Sublime, the Magnificent.[111]

• 2 •

حَسْبِيَ اللهُ وَنِعْمَ الْوَكِيل، نِعْمَ الْمَوْئَى وَنِعْمَ النَّصِير

*Ḥasbiyal-lāhu wa ni'mal-wakīl, ni'mal-mawlā wa
ni'man-naṣīr.*

Sufficient for me is Allah, the Best Guarantor, the Best
Protector, and the Best Helper.[112]

• 3 •

يَا حَيُّ يَا قَيُّومُ بِرَحْمَتِكَ نَسْتَغِيثُ أَغِثْنَا

Yā ḥayyu yā qayyūmu biraḥmatika nastaghīthu aghithnā

O Living, O All-Sustaining, we ask You through Your mercy for Your help, so help us![113]

• 4 •

لَا إِلَهَ إِلَّا أَنْتَ سُبْحَانَكَ إِنِّي كُنْتُ مِنَ الظَّالِمِين

Lā ilāha illā anta subḥānaka innī kuntu minadh-dhālimīn

There is no God but You, glory be to You, truly I have been of those who do wrong.[114]

• 5 •

سَلَامٌ قَوْلًا مِّن رَّبٍّ رَّحِيم

Salāmun qawlam-mir-rabbir-raḥīm

"Peace," a declaration from a Merciful Lord.[115]

• 6 •

لَيْسَ لَهَا مِنْ دُونِ اللهِ كَاشِفَة

Laysa lahā min dūnil-lāhi kāshifah

No one less than God can lift this. [116]

• 7 •

الصَّلَاتُ وَالسَّلَامُ عَلَيْكَ يَا سَيِّدِي يَا رَسُولَ اللهِ، ضَاقَتْ حِيلَتِي وَأَنْتَ
وَسِيلَتِي، أَدْرِكْنَا سَرِيعًا بِعِزَّةِ اللهِ

Aṣ-ṣalātu was-salāmu ‘alayka yā sayyidī yā rasūlal-lāh, ḍāqat ḥīlatī wa anta wasīlatī, adriknā sarī‘an bi ‘izzatillāh

Salutations and peace upon you, O leader of ours, O Messenger of Allah! I am helpless and you are my aid. With the power of Allah may we be like those who were rescued swiftly by you before they lost their way.

Endnotes

1   Qur'ān (2:186)

2   Al-Tirmidhī

3   Al-Tirmidhī

4   Qur'ān (7:55)

5   Al-Bukhārī

6   Muslim

7   Al-Tirmidhī

8   Al-Tirmidhī

9   Qur'ān (11:52)

10   Qur'ān (2:152)

11   Qur'ān (40:60)

12   Qur'ān (39: 53)

13   Qur'ān (4:142)

14   Qur'ān (39:22)

15   Muslim

16   Ibn al-Mubārak, *Kitāb al-Zuhd*

17   Aḥmad

18   Al-Bazzār

19   Qur'ān (4:103)

20   Al-Ṭabarānī

21   Ibn Abī Shaybah

22   Al-Ṭabarānī

23 Qur'ān (4:29)

24 Al-Bukhārī

25 Al-Ṭabarānī

26 Al-Tirmidhī

27 Aḥmad

28 Al-Bukhārī

29 Al-Bukhārī

30 Muslim

31 Muslim

32 Attributed to 'Alī ibn Abī Ṭālib (*Nahj al-Balāghah*)

33 Ibn Mājah

34 Al-Tirmidhī

35 Al-Ṭabarānī

36 Attributed to 'Urwa ibn al-Zubayr (narrated by al-Ḍiyā' al-Maqdisī, *al-'Udda li-l-karbi wa-l-shidda*).

37 Muslim

38 Attributed to 'Abd al-'Azīz al-Dīrīnī

39 Attributed to Prophet Ya'qūb by Dhū al-Nūn al-Miṣrī

40 Famously known as the ṣalāt al-ṭibbiyya (the ṣalāt of healing)

41 Al-Tirmidhī

42 Qur'ān (21:87)

43 Al-Bukhārī

44 Al-Bukhārī

45 The famous grammarian al-Aṣma'ī said, 'I envied 'Abd al-Malik ibn Marwān' (the Umayyad Caliph) for these words he uttered before his death.

46 Attributed to Prophet Dāwūd (Ibn Rajab, *Jāmi' al-'ulūm wa-l-ḥikam*)

47 Attributed to Abū Bakr al-Warrāq

48 Attributed to the tābi' al-tābi'īn 'Umar ibn Dharr

49 Supplication of Al-Qāḍī Shaydhala, as heard by his student Shahda

al-Kātiba (al-Dhahabī, *Tārīkh al-Islām*)

50 Supplication of the tābi'ī 'Awn ibn 'Abdullāh (Abū Nu'aym, *Ḥilyat al-awliyā'*)

51 Attributed to 'Abd al-'Azīz al-Dīrīnī

52 Al-Ṭabarānī (a supplication of the Prophet in 'Arafa)

53 Attributed to 'Abd al-'Azīz al-Dīrīnī

54 Attributed to Dhū al-Nūn al-Miṣrī

55 Attributed to 'Abd al-'Azīz al-Dīrīnī

56 Attributed to Imam Ja'far al-Ṣādiq (Al-Dhahabī, *Siyar a'lām al-nubalā'*)

57 Al-Daylamī, *Musnad al-Firdaws*

58 Attributed to Fatḥ al-Mawṣilī (Ibn Abī al-Dunyā, *Kitāb al-Riḍā 'an Allāh*)

59 Part of the famous 'Du'ā' al-Faraj' attributed to one of the pious, quoted in al-Ghazālī's *Iḥyā'* and elsewhere

60 Attributed to 'Alī ibn Abī Ṭālib (*Nahj al-Balāgha*)

61 Attributed to Ibrāhīm al-Taymī (al-Ghazālī, *Iḥyā' 'ulūm al-dīn*)

62 Qur'ān (39:36)

63 Al-Bukhārī

64 Qur'ān (7:196)

65 Abū Dāwūd

66 Abū Dāwūd

67 Muslim

68 Al-Bukhārī

69 Abū Dāwūd

70 Attributed to Prophet 'Īsā, (al-Bayhaqī, *Shu'ab al-Īmān*)

71 Muslim

72 Attributed to Ibn 'Abbās (Ibn Abī Shaybah, *al-Muṣannaf*)

73 Attributed to Abū Ḥayyān al-Tawḥīdī

74 Abū Dāwūd

75 First line from al-Ghazālī in his *Iḥyā*. Second line from Imam
Sufyān al-Thawrī, who attributed it to the salaf (the early generations of Muslims).

76 Taken from the du'ā' of Abū al-Dardā' who used to say, 'O Allah,
truly I seek refuge in You that I should do a deed which would
shame 'Abdullāh ibn Rawāḥah' (Nu'aym ibn Ḥammād, *Zawā'id
Kitāb al-Zuhd*). It was Ibn Rawāḥah who guided Abū al-Dardā' to
Islam.

77 Attributed to Ibn Shihāb al-Zuhrī (al-Dhahabī, *Siyar a'lām
al-nubalā'*)

78 Muslim

79 Qur'ān (2: 201)

80 Attributed to Shurayh ibn al-Ḥārith al-Qāḍī

81 Aḥmad

82 Abū Dāwūd

83 Attributed to Ibn 'Abbās (narrated by al-Bukhārī, *al-Adab
al-Mufrad*)

84 Qur'ān (40:44)

85 Qur'ān (27:62)

86 Attributed to Ṣāliḥ al-Murrī, a famous preacher from the tābi'
al-tabi'īn.

87 Al-Tirmidhī

88 In reference to Qur'ān (6:54)

89 Attributed to the chief judge al-Ḥārith ibn Miskīn

90 Sometimes attributed to Prophet Yūsuf when he was in the well

91 Attributed to a pious woman from the tābi'īn (Abū Bakr al-Dīnawrī,
Kitāb al-mujālasa wa jawāhir al-'ilm)

92 Attributed to Abū al-Ḥasan al-Shādhilī

93 Attributed to Abū Ḥayyān al-Tawḥīdī

94 Attributed to the Abbasid Caliph Hārūn al-Rashīd during the
Pilgrimage (al-Ṭabarī, *Tārīkh*). Elsewhere attributed to Wahb ibn

Munabbih, having found it in earlier texts (Abū Bakr al-Dīnawrī, *Kitāb al-mujālasa wa jawāhir al-ʿilm*).

95 Attributed to Muḥammad al-Bāqir (al-Ibshīhī, *al-Mustaṭraf*)

96 Al-Tirmidhī, except 'the companionship of the prophets.'

97 Attributed to al-Ḥakam ibn ʿUtayba, from the tābiʿ al-tābiʿīn (Maʿmar, *al-Jāmiʿ*)

98 Aḥmad

99 Abū Dāwūd

100 Al-Tirmidhī

101 Al-Tirmidhī

102 Abū Dāwūd

103 Attributed to Prophet Danyāl (Ibn Abī al-Dunyā, *al-Faraj baʿd al-Shidda*)

104 Famously known as the ṣalāt al-ṭibbiyya (the ṣalāt of healing)

105 Reference to Qurʾān (19:23)

106 Muslim. ʿĀʾisha, the wife of the Prophet ﷺ, overheard him ﷺ saying this supplication whilst in prostration during the night.

107 Al-Bukhārī

108 Abū Dāwūd. One of the female Companions of the Prophet ﷺ, Asmāʾ bint ʿUmays, said that the Prophet ﷺ taught her these words to say in times of distress. The great Caliph ʿUmar ibn ʿAbd al-ʿAzīz would repeat these words 7 times in times of difficulty.

109 Al-Bukhārī

110 Abū Dāwūd

111 Abū Dāwūd

112 Al-Bukhārī

113 Al-Tirmidhī

114 Qurʾān (21:87)

115 Qurʾān (36:58)

116 Qurʾān (53:58)

www.ingramcontent.com/pod-product-compliance
Lightning Source LLC
Chambersburg PA
CBHW031346060726
47590CB00007B/2649